SAVING THE SITUATION

SAVING THE SITUATION
The Battered Man's Handbook

First Published by The Family Practice Press 1996
Tel: + 44 (0)207 610 5520

2nd edition printed 2018

© Julian Nettlefold 1996

Julian Nettlefold asserts the moral right to be identified as Editor
of this book

A catalogue record for this book is available from the British
Library

Paperback ISBN 978-1-9999772-2-1
Ebook ISBN 978-1-9999772-3-8

Edited by Julian Nettlefold

With contributions from:
Wendy Holton
The Chemical Dependency Centre
Alicia Trevor
Susan Balfour
Hilary Halpin

Foreword by Baroness Lucy Faithfull OBE

Printed and bound in Great Britain by TJ International Ltd, Padstow, Cornwall

The Author - Julian Nettlefold

In the years 1980-1982, Julian Nettlefold ran a marketing company for engineering and defence equipment. He joined Defence magazine in 1982 to write articles on military vehicles. He also managed *Owners* a Horse racing publication. He launched Defence Industry Digest in 1984 to give information to the City and industry on all defence matters. The publication grew to take on a full-time editor, John Reed. Pearson Longman made an offer for the publication which was subsequently sold to them in August 1985.

From 1984-7 Julian Nettlefold was a member of the Bow Group Defence Committee where he was part of the team providing successful conferences on Procurement, SDI and European defence issues.

Prior to selling Defence Industry Digest, Julian Nettlefold formed Sky-Net Public Relations in 1984, a company specialising in Public Relations for the defence industry.

Julian Started the Family Practice Press in 1996 to address a crying need for reference books for men in difficult relationships.

In 1997 Julian Nettlefold started BATTLESPACE, a defence technology news service, it is extant.

Since the tragic murder of his son Harry in 2011, Julian also breeds racehorses, the first progeny being *'Harry The Norseman'* By *'Norse Dancer'* Out of *'Titled Lady'* Julian's mare.

Dedications

This book is dedicated to Harry whose good humour, bravery and sense of fun endured throughout my divorce ordeal. Tragically, as events will show, (In *Trial By Deceit*, to be published) he was cruelly murdered on August 27th 2011.

I would also like to thank those many experts who helped us to cope with the situation I found myself in in 1990, without them I would not have been able to cope with what happened in 2011, thus the abusers would have won, and the true nature of Harry's abuse and death covered up for ever. One of the most dreadful revelations in my research into Harry's death which will be shown in my forthcoming book *Trial By Deceit*, was that his murder involved people I had known and loved for many years.

I am indebted to Baroness Faithfull, who died in March 1996, in agreeing to write the foreword. I will never forget the day she drove up to London in 1996 to attend the launch of Saving The Situation at the Harbour Club. At the end of my talk she said, *"Even I didn't know how bad things were, you are going to see the Lord Chancellor tomorrow."* We went to see Lord Mackay and he ignored everything we told him.

With special thanks to Gerry Bermingham, former MP for St Helens, now working as a barrister, whose efforts in the House of Commons have brought a new understanding to problems within the divorce system.

I would also like to thank the other experts who have contributed to this book but who have no chapter especially Peter Alexander of Dawson & Co who contributed so much to the legal aspects of Chapter 11, Roland Powell who contributed so much to Chapter 1 and Dr Malcolm George who contributed to Chapter 2. Sadly, Malcom died in 2012 after a short fight against cancer. I last time I saw Malcolm was in hospital the day before he died, his parting words to me were, *"They must hate you as every time they kick you, you get stronger, keep fighting."* Sadly, at his funeral I was not allowed to praise what marvellous work he had done for the battered man.

The other fact which I find very worrying and disheartening is that society, Parliament and the legal profession, have learned nothing from the work which we and many others did in the 1990s. Men are still losing contact with their children and children like Harry continue to be abused by their mothers just making the list of Baby 'P' Victoria Climbie and others longer.

I often describe the period between 1980 and 2000 as a *'Holocaust against men and their children.'* So, for Parliament and the legal profession to admit this would mean paying huge amounts of compensation to men and their children as happened in Germany post-1945, so string it out until we are dead. I have very little doubt this is why the legal professions' self-funding insurance company the Solicitors Indemnity Fund (SIF) was wound up in the 1990s and why the profession tried to bankrupt me in 1996, as will be discussed in Trial By Deceit. Having sued two firms of lawyers, one twice, I was told by a member of FNF that I had got further than any man in suing his lawyer for negligence. That cover-up and concealment of vital evidence to prevent me winning cost Harry his life. Thus it appears that all concerned were prepared to allow Harry to be abused and killed to *'protect the system.'* As I write the reason for his death is still suicide rather than murder, accordingly everyone is hell bent on stopping the truth coming out.

For those of you who need a reference I can recommend the excellent BBC film *Conspiracy* about the Wansee Conference – I will say no more, apart from the fact that I believe that lawyers should lose the franchise to run Family Law in the UK.

The disgraceful rise in false rape allegations in 2017 only goes to show how an abusive system can adapt to target a new segment of vulnerable men, many of them who have had their lives ruined in the process, as happened to us husbands in the 1990s.

Given the time which has elapsed since the first publication in 1996 some of the authors may have moved on or sadly died and some organisations such as the Divorce Conciliation Service closed; a good start is to contact Relate.

I welcome the publication of this Handbook, which comes at an opportune moment in answer to a crying need.

Long experience has shown me that many married couples have recourse to divorce too quickly and too easily. Had they been prepared to work hard at their relationship, for the sake of the children if for no other reason, I suggest that many marriages might have been saved. Children take their standards, and learn what is right and wrong, from both parents as a united couple. They suffer greatly if one of these parents leaves home, particularly if the absentee is blamed openly for the break-up of the union.

It is not always the husband who leaves home or is solely responsible for the break-up; in our sympathy for the abandoned mother, we sometimes tend to forget those fathers who are left to bring up their children without a mother's help. We also overlook the sorrow of a father living apart from his children.

The general situation would be easier if couples recognised that the well being of children should surely come first and that each parent, the father as well as the mother, has a significant influence in the upbringing of the children, their moral standards, their attitude to life and their happiness.

The marital relationship is highly complex; many factors are involved and interests which may conflict. Marriage is a matter of give and take, something that calls for sustained and patient effort by both partners, for restraint and for cool, considered judgement. Unfortunately, the situation created when a marriage begins to show signs of disruption is fraught with bitterness and emotional stress, leading to headstrong and impulsive action.

This Handbook is valuable because it recognises that an unhappy marriage has many facets and gives rise to several problems. The different chapters deal faithfully with each of these. It comes to the rescue of fathers whose contribution is sometimes undervalued. This Handbook could be of considerable help to fathers in distress.

Baroness Lucy Faithfull OBE- 26th December 1910 – 13th March 1996

After her education Lucy Faithfull worked at Birmingham Settlement for three years until 1935 running clubs and acting as a caseworker. She entered subsequently the education department of the London County Council as a care committee organiser. During the Second World War and until 1948, she served as a regional welfare officer for the evacuee programme. In the following decade she became employed as an inspector in the children's department of the Home Office. Faithfull joined the Oxford City Council in 1958 as one of the first children's officers. She was appointed its Director of Social Services in 1970, retiring four years later. In the New Year's Honours 1972, she was awarded an Officer of the Order of the British Empire. Four years later, in 1976, Margaret Thatcher offered her a seat in the House of Lords and after an initial refusal she accepted a life peerage with the title Baroness Faithfull, of Wolvercote, in the County of Oxfordshire on 26 January. In the House, she was instrumental in the passing of the Children Act 1989. She helped to establish and from 1995 chaired the All Party Parliamentary Group for Children. She was a vociferous opponent of Home Secretary, Michael Howard's Criminal Justice and Public Order Bill of 1994 which proposed the establishment of secure *'training centres'* in the grounds of adult prisons for children aged between 12 and 14, arguing that locking up children is ineffective and that the huge cost of these could be better spent intervening with families at an earlier stage.

She was trustee of a number of voluntary organisations, notably the Caldecott Community, and Bessels Leigh schools. Vice-president of the National Association of Voluntary Hostels from 1978 and of Barnardo's from 1989. Faithfull supported the National Children's Bureau, of which she was president. In 1993 she founded the Lucy Faithfull Foundation, which works as a child protection agency helping sexually abused children and their families. She died unmarried in London in 1996.
(Source: Wikipedia)

Contents

These chapters examine the problems of relationships and they enable the reader to get a better understanding of the problem he faces and whether it is biological, social or related to external forces such as stress, alcohol or drugs.

PART II - EXPERT HELP

These chapters will enable you to find expert solutions to your problems within the marriage.

PART III - SELF HELP

These chapters give some helpful advice how to manage your life whilst your relationship is in turmoil. If you have decided to end the relationship, then good health is essential to enable you to think straight and brief the necessary experts. These chapters will limit the damage caused by divorce or upheaval and help you to start a new life.

PREFACE

When I wrote *Saving The Situation* in 1996 I found myself in a position where I had been happily married with a young child one minute and then, after hoping that my wife would recover from her violent outbursts exhibited after the birth of my son, to one of being out on the street falsely accused of being a wife beater. In short I was framed by my wife whilst trying to defend my son. This event is covered in greater detail in my next book *Trial By Deceit*. Leaving Harry my son in the care of a violent woman who not only beat me up but also my Harry, then aged 18 months. I was very lucky in finding help from people who understood my plight, unlike many men who either die or live the rest of their lives in penury having lost contact with their children.

I decided to reprint the book in 2018 whilst still investigating the murder of my darling son Harry because it was apparent that nothing had changed since 1996 and there were men being accused of rape and domestic violence when in fact they were either innocent or the victim.

When we saw Lord Mackay, the Lord Chancellor in 1996, at the invitation of Baroness Faithfull, we outlined the seriousness of the situation that men and their children were in. We had estimated that as many as 100,000 men had been forced out of their homes under false allegations of violence. This process always resulted in the family home being sold and the lawyers pocketing £2 billion a year in the process.

During the 2011 riots in the UK, David Cameron used the figure of 100,000 to outline the problem. I happened to point out to him by email that we told the government that figure in 1996.

One noticeable omission in the new issue is the Chapter on male helplines. I worked with Les Davidson of the Merton M.A.L.E. helpline, but this was closed in 1996. There are few male helplines available now, huge loss to men in difficult situations.

The fact that in 2016 there were 106,959 divorces of opposite-sex couples in 2016, an increase of 5.8 per cent compared with 2015, with men and women getting divorced at a rate of 8.9 per 1,000 married people - up 4.7 per cent, has done nothing to deter people from entering this great institution. The realisation that you may become a statistic on your wedding day is as far from your mind as it could be. You have met the person you love and want to be with for the rest of your life; you are the happiest couple in the world and no one has ever felt as much in love as you do. When the problems in a marriage occur, they do so very suddenly and unless they are dealt with quickly the matter can boil over into divorce proceedings, solicitors, unhappiness, single parents and confused children.

If you are a man who has suddenly confronted a serious situation in his marriage or relationship where the only way out appears to be leaving your partner, divorce and the destruction of your relationship or family, stop and consider the consequences. At the moment, as in 1996, there is little help for a man in a difficult relationship, the various agencies appointed to deal with problems are not trained to counsel men with violent, alcoholic or difficult wives or partners; the only two options advised are for a man to live with the problem, leave the relationship and where required divorce. In the case of divorce a lawyer is required to 'tick the box in the Application Form,' that he or she has recommended counselling, but few do, as counselling might deny them their huge fees and access to the family home. Divorce will not help the children and will certainly not help the man as statistics on male suicide amply demonstrate. If you are in a relationship that has lasted over two years, your partner is entitled to a share of your assets, including the family home. Unfortunately, the last stop has to be the law and solicitors. Even if you do manage to stem the problem by the use of the law the damage will have been done as the hatred and mistrust created is enough on its own to destroy any relationship.

As parents we have a responsibility to our children and we must do the most we can to preserve the family unit. If both parties work together to solve the problem, then once you have come through it and out the other side you will thank God that you did not take the path of divorce.

This book is designed to give a man the ability to solve family problems before they destroy him and his family. Should divorce, or the end of the relationship, be the recommended way then he should have a fairer say and understanding in the divorce proceedings to gain him custody or fair access to his children. At the moment the perception of family problems are biased towards the wife or female partner. If we can instil a degree of understanding of women's problems and at the same time convince the system that as men we can look after children then the system should be fairer and men should play a greater role.

The government is currently attempting to halt a large rise in juvenile crime; statistics show us that the absence of a father figure in the household is a great contributor to that problem. The fact that 84% of the children involved in 2011 UK riots had no fathers clearly showed the depth of the problem. If the wife or girlfriend is suffering from PND, alcoholism or depression a far better way should be for that person to be helped and the husband look after the children whilst she is recovering. The last thing we need is for a woman who is sick from depression, alcoholism or PMS to be left with children which she cannot look after and leave them to their own devices on the street. The biggest problem facing society, as I found, is how to deal with a mother with a Personality Disorder. Currently she has to kill or maim the child before the father gets custody as it is deemed anti-social to label the woman with the nomenclature '*Personality Disorder*,' up to the crime she gets the label '*Suspected Personality Disorder.*'

In my discussions with members of Families Need Fathers I have found couples who time and time again were driven to divorce and regretted it later. Should the wife or husband need help then let's find it within the marriage and give the father custodial rights to look after his children where necessary. After all, we all feel unwell at some point in our lives, but we must not allow that illness to destroy all that we have worked to establish.

In conversation with Dr Dalton, the pioneer of PMS and Wendy Holton her daughter founder of PMS Help, they told me that Dr Dalton had offered to lecture the Law Society on the problems women face after childbirth and how they should not be allowed to divorce until at least a year after the birth; no interest was registered. Dr Dalton's PMS Help is a prime example of how marriages can be helped as she has demonstrated that at least 50% of her patients are brought to her by their husbands. Once they admit the problem the marriage survives.

Saving the Situation

Each chapter of this book is designed to help you with the specific problem you are facing, don't forget you may be the problem so examine yourself as well.

All the case studies in this book are real, but the names and places have been changed.

Chapter 1

The Most Remarkable Woman I Have Ever Met

"If any faculty of our nature may be called more wonderful than the rest, it is memory...the memory is sometimes so retentive, so serviceable, so obedient; at others, so bewildered and so weak; and at others again, so tyrannic, so beyond control." Jane Austen

Psychology Today magazine described Neuro Linguistic Programming (NLP) as *"the most powerful vehicle for change in existence"*. Co-developer Richard Bandler described NLP thus:

> *"NLP is an attitude based on curiosity about people and an approach to others that considers each experience a rare and unprecedented opportunity to learn; it is methodology...a way of thinking about and studying people and the process of communication; it is a technology...a range of specific techniques that allows you to organise your perceptions and behaviour to get well-defined and ecologica results."*

And, as Arthur C Clarke wrote: *"Any sufficiently developed technology is indistinguishable from magic."*

When I wrote *Saving the Situation* in 1996 I was still oblivious as to why I had landed myself and Harry in the situation we were in. I appeared to come from a normal family, albeit that my father was disabled, I came from a wealthy background, I had a brother and a sister and had been privately educated at the top English Public School, Eton. I knew that I had fractured my jaw as a baby but had been told by my mother that I had banged it on the pram. The fact that I had been assaulted by my mother was a fact which I never considered until I met Dr Hetty MacKinnon in 1997.

There is little doubt that, if I had not met Hetty, my life would not have changed in the dramatic way in which it did.

I read an article in the Daily Mail in 1995 by Anna Pukas about the effects of the truth drug on patients. I rang Anna and said that I would like to meet her, as my sister was given the truth drug in her early teens. Anna put me in touch with a lady called Vera Diamond in London whom I went to see. As I was at the time in the process of moving to Scotland, Vera recommended I contact Dr Hetty MacKinnon in Glasgow for further research into the subject; Hetty later informed me that Vera has since passed away.

It latterly transpired that my darling sister Tessa who died in 2003, aged 53, had been sexually abused by my father and others since about the age of eleven.

When I went to meet Hetty in 1997, I was greeted by a woman who immediately commanded my attention and instilled confidence in me. She appeared as the archetypical Glasgow G.P., small in stature, well dressed in a neat tweed skirt, with a softly spoken voice which had a hint of the steel I would soon find. We discussed her background and her theories.

She had started life as a GP and then become a Police Doctor and thus had experienced first hand a great number of traumatic events surrounding people being taken into custody. She told me about her research into Neuro-Linguistic Programming (NLP), an art developed for cleaning the brain of legacy thought patterns.

I left her thinking that she would be of great use for a future book, little knowing that a year later she would change my life forever.

In January 1998, during the preparation process for the Final Hearing after Harry's Statement of Abuse to East Lothian Police and subsequent Initial Court Hearing, I rang Hetty in great distress as, not for the first time, I had been labelled obsessive and delusional. She saw me and we discussed the Court process given her experience in Court matters as a Police Surgeon. She said that the job of the barrister cross-examining me was to keep my attention so that he could break me down. She told me to move my head from the barrister to the Judge, as required by the Court, to answer any question that would disarm both of them, it did!

She then suggested that I saw London psychiatrist Dr Willy Monteiro for a second opinion as to my true state of mind. I had heard that he was a psychiatrist to the rich and famous and my day was made when I saw coming out of his surgery the patients who had been before me, Rod Stewart and his wife Rachel Hunter, I was lost for words with her beauty and striking good looks and wondered why on earth he was divorcing her! After two gruelling appointments, Willy wrote a Report supporting my concerns for Harry.

At a later appointment Hetty said to me, *"They've found your weak point,"* to which I replied, *"I haven't got one."* Her response took me aback, *"Do you mind if I give you hypnosis and regress you to birth?"*

"Of course," I said, trying to hide any anxiety I was feeling, *"Anything to help the case for Harry."*

She put me under and counted forwards the months since birth. When we got to nine months she stopped and asked, *"How are you feeling?"* I said that I felt nervous and she continued to month seventeen, at which point my whole body went rigid.

She asked me what I saw.

My reply was, *"The hands came towards me and an electric shock went through my body."*

Not commenting immediately, Hetty said that she would continue with the journey forward through my life and the same thing happened again when reached the point where I was twenty three months old.

She asked me what I thought I had seen and I told her that as a child I had fractured my jaw in my pram. My mother had told me for years that I had banged it on the pram when in fact she had assaulted me. Forty five minutes later, having replaced this vision with a picture of Harry, the demons present in my body since the age of seventeen months were banished, and along with them the power of Sophie to control my life. It also limited the Court's ability to exploit my weaknesses to *'win'* the Case.

In a bizarre turn of events, after years of problems with my ears, having gone deaf in my right ear aged 60, I was told by my GP that he couldn't see my right ear drum! He referred me to a specialist who said that I may have a fractured the petrous bone in my ear when my mother hit me.

I asked Hetty if I should tell my mother. She said, *"No, she will know."* That was perfectly true as Mum and I had a much better relationship until the day she died.

She said that Sophie, when she married me, had spotted instinctively my weakness as a victim, and that now the control process was over and I could live life properly. She said that the body has two strands of electricity, the high voltage circuit which controls the body movements and the low which controls feelings and the sub-conscious. She said that what had happened when Sophie assaulted Harry and I was that it kicked in the sub-conscious abuse I had suffered in my pram and thus I dealt with the adult abuse as that little child I was at the time. The other problem we had was that Sophie appeared too cool under cross-examination of the abuse; thus, I was deemed to be *'delusional'* as she looked so pretty and cool!

Sophie is very pretty and charming and used both these assets to disarm the people in authority, a common facet of such people. As Malcolm George, who taught me about Personality Disorder and how to combat it, rightly put it, *"Experts rely on stereotypes."*

When he saw Sophie in the Witness Box in the High Court in 2006, he took me to one side and said, *"You've got a real problem!"* *"Why?"* I asked. *"She's the best I have ever seen!"*

After the treatment, a friend of mine saw me after many years and commented how much calmer I was than ten years previously – demons banished! He had observed that I flinched when I saw certain ladies, a habit I hadn't even noticed!

I could then look back on my life and understand why I had married Sophie and how, whatever I did, I would have ended in a similar situation. The weirdest part is my interest in 'things Australian' at my prep school, as if my life had been mapped out for me!

So, for any man who needs to understand his current situation and link it to his upbringing and past, I can do no more than recommend NLP. Dr Keith Stoll had already told me in 1990 to be careful about remarrying as I would repeat the pattern.

When I was cured by the NLP from Hetty it also disarmed Sophie's ability to control me. She did not know I had been cured and when Harry was murdered she used the usual provocation which I had resisted for years to no avail. That was the beginning of the end for her and her husband.

Chapter 2

Recognising Problems in Your Relationship

The search for the *'safe space'* of a quality relationship in which we can emotionally invest is now an important feature of all our lives. Relationships are now of such importance that they occupy an ever increasing space in our society and culture. As with all important aspects of our lives industries have sprung up specialising in relationships from agony aunts through to lawyers, therapists and social workers. Women are the main target for this industry for the simple reason that women are openly interested in their relationships. The benefit gained by women from this information can be seen by the enormous coverage of relationship aspects in women's literature, books, magazines, the woman's section of newspapers, TV and Radio which cover every aspect of relationships. Having said that the role models that women are expected to live up to creates problems in their own lives if they are not as lithe as Claudia Schiffer or as efficient as Margaret Thatcher and as warm as Lorraine Kelly.

I was the star of the show on Thames TV in when Lorraine Kelly interviewed me about the abuse I had suffered. She was so kind and understanding and put me at my ease.

Saving the Situation

The interview was so popular that Thames had to reshow it later.

Similar media resources for men are less well developed reflecting the misinformed view that men are less interested in their emotional lives and relationships thus reading about men's relationships as a man may be a new experience. The growth in new publications such as *Men's Health* shows a growing trend to men's interest magazines. Reading about relationships is a challenge worth taking up that will enrich the way men think and feel about their emotional experiences.

For most men the relationship with their partner and children is the centre of their lives and their biggest emotional investment. Most men will make sure that he is well informed before buying a property, shares or a car; this chapter is an introduction to a man's biggest investment, his emotional investments, the consequences of them going wrong will change his life for ever. We spend a lot of time looking after our other investments so a continuing understanding of the most fluid of investments is critical to a man and his family's stability.

What maintains a quality relationship can only be answered by the couple who experience their relationship in meeting both their needs and expectations. Whilst general advice can be given about how not to make a relationship a disaster, generalisations often fail to pinpoint the exact problem within the relationship which may be affected by an outside source such as stress or PMS. There is no instant therapeutic technology that will repair all poor quality relationships because it is one area where the characters, qualities and personalities of individual people still matter. If you are experiencing problems in your relationship read on.

Although more men are expressing their emotions and attempting to reclaim their right to care, men are frequently inhibited by the need to conform to a masculine stereotype which pressures them to remain emotionally silent. This oppressive silence makes it harder for men to check out if their expectations of relationships are realistic. The negative images of what it is to be a man asserted by both establishment and feminist critics of masculinity converge in a surprising way to create a situation in which men have to continually prove that they are emotionally competent and caring.

Many writers in the relationship industry feel safe in claiming that women are more in touch with their emotions than men, there are good reasons for doubting this claim; emotional stereotyping is a major problem for men. Men's emotions are under-valued in our society where women are seen as emotionally expressive and competent. What a man needs to know is that his partner feels the same but expresses her emotions in a different way using different language.

Both partners may be expressing emotions generated by the world outside the relationship, importing anger and frustration into what should be a safe high quality space. The world of work places a high value on emotions that are incorrectly seen as masculine such as toughness, single-mindedness, drive, ruthlessness, objectivity and so on. If either partner brings these performance oriented relationship styles home a low quality relationship will be in the making. Recent research shows that the styles of thinking and feeling men and women develop at work have a powerful impact in other aspects of their lives, so men should be aware that so called masculine influences can be brought into the relationship by their female partner.

Men value their relationships as highly as women but more frequently tolerate a poor quality relationship more readily than women. This *'inaction man'* attitude may explain why it is women who initiate 75% of divorces in the UK. More men regret the breakdown of a relationship than women and in many relationships, it is the woman's feeling which are the main deciding factor in whether the relationship continues; with the male partner more frequently having to leave the home whether he wants to or not. Men in good quality relationships benefit from better psychological and physical health than men in poor quality ones, men who have failed relationships or are divorced suffer significantly from poor health. If ultimately the female partner becomes the major carer you will be emotionally excluded from caring and nurturing your children. Men maintain the stereotypical macho image of masculinity that causes them so much pain by staying silent about the emotional consequences that this exclusion from caring and the breakdown of relationships causes them.

The Myth of the man as powerful individuals is simply a Myth, what he has to lose is virtually everything he values including his health. Life means change and as relationships are very much alive they will change over time so, a relationship which begins meeting the needs and expectations of both partners will change as new needs and expectations arise either because of changes in the individual people or life events such as unemployment, childbirth or a change in one or both partners values and beliefs. It is an illusion to believe that anything other than hard work and continual emotional maintenance work will give a man and his partner the relationship he requires.

Some potential pain generators are explored below.

Illusions and Disillusion

Acceptance as a lover, a partner and as a special man, enhances a man's life and generates a variety of emotions such as elation, joy and passion. This heady emotional high is not on its own a sound basis for a lasting relationship. Emotions are powerful, a man can fall in love with the emotions and it is the feelings not the person he desires so that when only the person is left he wonders what has changed, simply the way he feels. The illusion that this emotional high will make our lives better can lead men, and women, into marriage, parenthood and other long term commitments. To some extent men and their partners will have been influenced in making sense of their own personal story by popular media and the relationship industry which has deluged singles, lovers and couples with advice stories and statistics about how difficult it is to find 'love' with the emphasis on sexuality and commonality. Emotions are seen as more important than any other aspect of the relationship and the main images portrayed are those of romantic happiness or abusive hell. Every relationship is based on some sort of contract whether formalised as marriage or not. The main content of the relationship such as how and to what extent that relationship can meet each partners' needs and expectations is frequently ignored.

As children, we are educated in maths, science, languages, economics and other subjects but crucially, how to manage life after school is not on the curriculum, so when problems happen, we are powerless to understand what is happening and how to tackle them. In addition, as in my case there were demons buried deep in my psyche that drew me to marry an abusive woman. You accept what you are born into and accept any dysfunctionality. It took me to the age of 60 to understand the truly dysfunctional nature of my family and the fact that my poor darling Harry was the fall guy for all those years of dysfunctionality. In short, I had unknowingly married my mother and came to accept the abuse metered out by my wife day in day out. Abusers are very confident, cunning and perceptive people, they can spot a victim a mile off and use it to their advantage. They don't pick someone who will fight back as they want to dominate the relationship.

When a number of us Battered Husbands were invited on to the Kirsty Young Show in Glasgow in 1995, to discuss Battered Husbands, six of us, all about my size, 5ft 11ins and well built, (five of us had boxed for our school), were put on the stage at the opening of the show. As the lights went up, there was complete silence as those burly Glaswegian men realised they were not alone! The STV switchboard was jammed with victims and the show closed early.

Disillusion in a relationship comes in stages and at first the man suffers quietly and privately as the joy of discovering the confirmation of being needed and desired fades, bleached by the dawning reality that his partner is just like him. His partner too has flaws, needs, expectations and is just as vulnerable to the big world outside the hoped for safe space of the relationship. As either or both see the failure of the idealised expectations a feeling of betrayal is experienced leading to a belief that the other partner has ceased caring. Conflicts are left unresolved as neither partner can feel understood by the other and this is the basis of the safe space each hoped for and expected. Once this mythical unity of body and soul is questioned we can look at our partner and ourselves in a more useful way accepting a satisfactory relationship and abandoning the search for the 'perfect' relationship.

Understanding problems

It helps to have a simple model for understanding relationships because even without children what goes on between partners within the boundaries of any relationship is complex. These patterns or relationship styles can be described using the familiar ideas of co operation and competition.

Wendy Holton describes in detail problems related to childbirth in Chapter 4. In a number of cases it has been found that following the birth of a child especially male, the father will often feel excluded from the loving relationship as a great deal of the love, care, time and affection will be going to the child. It is also very common for the couple's sex life to deteriorate at this time another source of frustration for the man.

Power Sharing

In a relationship, where both partners can share power and support one another, there is a recognition of their rights to be equal but different; both co-operate with one another with one partner giving up power to the other to help both meet their needs and expectations. Imbalance does not mean that one partner is less powerful than the other only that in a particular situation and time one partner has assumed a lead and the other has agreed and supports them taking a subordinate role. Real power imbalances will exist between partners but if the more powerful partner maintains the imbalance then the weaker partner will constantly attempt to find ways of reclaiming power even when they seem to accept the terms of the more powerful partner. The stronger partner will use control techniques to maintain dominance in the relationship which will run from emotional degradation to actual violence.

The key to achieving a mutually co-operative relationship style is choice and to make choice a reality there must be the flexibility to accept change. Both partners must allow the other to choose and support their choice even when that choice is to disagree. For example, as needs for closeness and intimacy change, expression of feelings between the partners may change but you can still give your partner the hugs and kisses she deserves and be a good listener. This style of relating is practical as it allows both partners the opportunity to do what they are good at for the benefit of both confirming their collective talents and minimising their collective weaknesses. This co-operative is the way to a safe quality relationship and beats competition at any price.

Competitive Relationship Style

Ideas of balance and equality are, like caring, highly valued ideals in our society and the competitive man is frequently portrayed as the ideal man. As more women have imported ideas from feminism and the relationship industry into relationships, women have in some ways taken on the competitive profile of the stereotypical man. The resulting competition for equal rights without a recognition of difference is sexist taking assumptions about men's power and male dominance for granted. Women are told that their *'oppression'* is caused solely by men and that they are victims. These ideas have become an additional problem in relationships and research indicates that where partners import these ideas into their relationships they have a negative effect. Competition to achieve predetermined expectations of balance or equality creates uncertainty because of the possibility of losing thus any competitive relationship will not give either partner a safe space. Where one or both partners need to be equal and achieve balance there will be constant opportunities to be equally defensive or equally aggressive, equally passive or equally active.

As a man you may adopt the co-operative, sharing style of the so-called *'new man,'* doing your share of domestic and emotional maintenance; but a competitive partner will point out your mistakes thus devaluing your efforts. When you care, your partner will try to care more or reject you as insincere. If you have a problem your partner will insist that their problem is worst devaluing your emotional needs by claiming that you are not meeting theirs. Passivity presented as incompetence or weakness can be a source of carefully maintained powerless dependency to get their partner to meet their needs in a manipulative, indirect way. This competitive *'neediness'* forces the other partner into a supportive role where the competition is to meet their partners' ever-present needs. In a competitive relationship there are no winners even when couples locked into this competitive style try to negotiate they tend to operate an exchange system where one partner or both will always try to get the best deal. Relationship boundaries, intimacy and power are difficult areas in any relationship but when one or both partners expects and needs to be in control the result will be emotional conflict and a low quality relationship that is potentially an abusive, unsafe space.

A competitive relationship can become a game without end

which will be impossible to work out as every aspect of the relationship can be turned into a contest. If you adopt an exaggerated male role to cope with a competitive partner you will escalate the relationship's competitive aspects. As a man you need to look carefully at the assumptions, values and beliefs on which your needs and expectations are based to see if you are recognising your partner's rights as being as important as your own. Your partner can be forced into a situation where they have to compete. If you are trying to dominate them but equally men with competitive partners will have to work hard to survive the relationship.

My parents' relationship was a mirror of this, with both of them choosing to control the other. My mother married a disabled man to control him but quickly realised that he was controlling her. I bought them a book on Co-Dependency called '*Co-Dependent No More*', I don't believe they ever read it.

Four Basic Assumptions in Relationship Styles

None of these styles is exclusive with all relationships but all contain some elements of each style.

Reciprocity

Each partner recognises the other's strengths and weaknesses and tries to find a fit with their own talents. You do what you can, and your partner does what they can, basic give and take. Both partners recognise that they have equal rights and responsibilities to each other including the work they will both need to do to maintain their relationship. This style of relationship is the most likely to maintain the quality of a relationship because it makes change easier and will meet most of both partners' expectations.

Exchange

In an exchange based relationship there is always an unanswered question which is, *'what's in it for me?'* The only rights here are those which can be secured through wheeling and dealing with one or both partners trying to get as much as they can. This style of relationship is competitive with continual possibilities of manipulation, argument and the denial of responsibility. Responsibility is denied by the claim that the other partner did not carry out a certain task or did not do it well enough you did not have to carry out your part of the agreement.

Altercentric

This other centred relationship style is more often found in parent child relationships where a parent lives for and sometimes through their child. In this relationship style one partner lives for the other always putting the other partner's needs first. The other centred partner believes that they have to constantly earn the safe space they need as they don't deserve to be cared for. If the absence of self-esteem of the alter centric partner fails to meet the other partner's expectations or causes them to feel overwhelmed and trapped by the altercentric partner's dependence, then a low quality relationship will be in the making.

Egocentric

We are all egocentric or self-centred to some extent, the presence of a sense of self and a strong, together personality, is a plus in a relationship for both partners. At its worst an egocentric relationship style is one where one or both partners put their own needs and expectations first.

If there is one partner who is more egocentric then they may reject or dominate the other partner if they feel that the relationship is preventing them meeting their needs. A relationship between two egocentric partners could work but would more probably become competitive at some point when one partner made demands on the other.

Domination and Abuse

Domination is not the preserve of men who tend to use direct ways of achieving domination. Women tend to use indirect ways of achieving the power to dominate their partners. Men can feel controlled or manipulated by a female partner but not understand the problem because as a man they assumed that they should be in control of their life. Domination involving physical, emotional, sexual, economic and psychological abuse are all possible in a relationship and all equally damaging. Domination is very different from simply being better or more successful in some area or other, domination is about control, denying choice, abusing a partner to the point where they are the victim. Strategies for domination usually cover all aspects of a relationship being both direct and indirect. As women tend to use indirect ways of dominating their partners, emotional and psychological abuse are more frequently used by female partners. For example, you may give way to a partner to show how much you care only to find that any attempt to assert yourself is met with violent outbursts and seen as proof that you do not really '*love*' her. In this exchange style relationship you are '*loved*' and valued on condition that you meet your partner's expectations and become altercentric. If you find that you are constantly forgiving and asking to be forgiven you need to look very carefully at what is going on before resentment and anger take over.

Your partner will be well aware of her own power as a woman and will often be skilled at presenting a *'good girl'* image while making your life unbearable. A typical strategy for emotional and psychological domination will begin by excluding you then devaluing you and in time you can find yourself the victim of an egocentric, abusive partner and well on the way to being dominated. Your partner can exploit the myths of masculinity to dominate you for example she can arouse you sexually but not allow you to make love, make it clear that she finds other men more attractive and that she has the sexual power to tum them on. Masculinity is always open to challenge so your status as a man can be devalued by your partner to hurt and degrade you using the stereotypes of what it is to be a *'real man'* knowing, as you do, that the myths are impossible expectations.

Emotional and psychological abuse can involve direct physical abuse, but men frequently refuse to admit that a physical attack by their partner has happened or that it is abuse. Women may attack a partner to cause physical damage but also put their male partner in a situation where he will have to be physically violent to defend himself; as the stereotype is that men are violent it is probably your female partner's story which will be believed.

Once the man is labelled as violent he will find that it is his partner who has the power because police, social services and the legal system will be on her side. Accusations of physical violence including sexual abuse can be used by the female to disempower, criminalise and exclude the man legally, socially and emotionally from everything the man values in the relationship.

If there is violence in the relationship or there is a potentially violent situation then you must seek help now because, do not forget that if you, as a man, lay one finger on your partner then yours and your children's lives will change forever.

Rejection and Being Rejected

Rejection is not a single act, not a single decision it happens slowly in stages as it is found more and more that the man's expectations are not being fulfilled, the rejection process begins. Initially dissatisfaction, a need to be emotionally or physically distant are needs that the man will feel without knowing exactly why. He may begin to ignore the areas in which his partner meets his expectations and needs and *'negatively'* monitor his partner only seeing where they fail to meet them. Values, beliefs and expectations change so if both partners do not find a way of responding to changes in each other what began as a good quality relationship may become a poor quality pain.

The work of building a safe space and supporting a family creates unexpected demands and needs. Many of the tasks are just hard work which without co-operation and commitment will be just grind you down wearing out quality and destroying pleasure, commitment and fun. You may even be rejected for being boring and not responding to your partner's desire for fun. Women who do not experience their relationship as supportive are at a great risk of suffering emotional distress such as anxiety and depression. The risk increases if the woman is mostly at home caring for children in a low quality relationship not yours. Values around parenting are changing but far too slowly and many men are effectively absent from the real caring role with their children.

Caring is demanding emotionally and physically, and men can develop as carers given the opportunity but as caring has been seen as a woman's role it has become feminised to the exclusion of men. The government has invested a lot of money in the image of the woman as the main carer and any attempt by men to disprove this theory must begin with the man proving that he is not the abusing drunken thug so often portrayed in the media and court. A better way of seeing mothering and fathering are as things we do in the style of a mother or a father. What this means is that men can care for children as well as a woman for example, changing nappies, giving bottles, playing, bathing and cuddling.

The roles of mother and father are important examples of the way society works to keep the roles of men and women separate but the reality is that as a man you can perform what is seen as a mothering role and equally a woman can perform a fathering role. The mother or father of any gender is the ideal of co-operative sharing in a relationship. In a quality relationship the man will be able to work out with his partner how to meet both theirs and their children's needs and expectations. Once the either partner has decided to end her relationship with her partner not her children the rejecting partner will work hard at excluding the other partner from caring for the children to discredit them as a parent and gain greater emotional attachment from the children.

One method of rejection is to deny the problems claiming your partner cannot understand what is wrong or can't talk about it. Your partner will be believed by others if she claims that you are unable to understand and don't talk about emotions. Rather than strive pointlessly in the hope of gaining some supportive approval get your partner to understand your feelings of rejection. You may expect your partner to understand your feelings but if the man depends on this stereotype he could be feeling the cold wind of rejection for some time to come.

Men respond in a different way to women regarding confiding relationships with their partners. Whilst women will be more open, a man will respond in a more private and silent way than women. Men usually disguise their feelings but show a greater level of physical arousal to emotional situations than women. Women usually talk about their feelings and can become dependent on having an audience to share their verbal expression and analysis of their emotional life. What a woman often needs is someone special to share her stories about her emotional experience and who will validate her own interpretation of her feelings. If you as the partner are that audience and you do not respond sympathetically you will be deemed as unsupportive. This emotional experience of rejection tells you that the relationship has a problem.

Sex, Love and Dangerousness

Men are stereotyped as either real men with an insatiable sex drive or wimps who cannot get it up. The relationship industry constructs images of men as sexually demanding emotional orphans and of women as wanting to relate more closely and emotionally than men thus drawing the conclusion that men want sex and women want emotionally fulfilling sexual intimacy. This conclusion is both sexist and misleading missing the point that men and women have different styles and repertoires. If both partners pursue their individual needs and desires then the stage is set for conflict, manipulations and a stressful unsafe low quality relationship where neither partner gets what they need.

Lack of sexual performance can be a great source of anxiety for men, statistics show that at least 5% of the male population have difficulty obtaining an erection. As a man you may experience hugs and cuddles as sexual *'come ons'* but for a woman these feelings can be different. Once sex, intimacy and affection are accepted into your safe space then you can both build a structure to meet your own needs and expectations. A co-operative approach to sexuality will answer most of your needs and enable you and your partner to overcome the unreliable information and experience that you have both brought into the relationship.

The man's concern for physical attractiveness as a main source of sexual arousal is another problem. Can he tell his partner that she doesn't turn him on any more or that he loves and wants to be with her but that sexually he is responding to another woman? Then look at yourself to see if you are still attractive to your partner. Women do not create an image just for their men but also to confirm their status amongst other women, the designer clothes industry confirms this. The powerful way in which women can present themselves shows up in relationships when a woman does not dress up at home but dresses to maximise her power and attractiveness when she goes out to work or play. Women's presentations send conflicting messages to men who are frequently less developed in terms of the *'social intelligence'* necessary to pick up and interpret behaviour than women. Men can be confused by the powerful images women can convey. No man is more confused than a neglected and frustrated partner who does not know what is going on or even that his partner has what amounts to an advantage in playing the game. If the man is not secure in his masculine identity it will be easy for his partner to tap into the problem to discredit him by attacking his self-image

23

and making him dependant on her assessment of his worth as a man. In a poor quality relationship, the man's sexual needs will be experienced by his partner as invasive and insincere demands and you will experience her as cold and unresponsive. Some sort of arrangement may be arrived at which results in mechanical sex, just going through the physical motions which results in both partners feeling let down, frustrated and used.

Male sexuality in the media is portrayed as dangerous rather than fragile and this construction of men as sexual predators can be used against the man by his partner who wants to get the man out of her life by making sexual allegations from rape, an affair, through to child molestation. The latter was a new form of accusation used in the Court to remove the father from the family home and from seeing his children under an Ouster, although this process is used less frequently. A very dangerous form of false accusation, like accusations of assault, the real victims are not protected as the allegations become a mechanism for the divorce process. In many cases the children may be brain washed by the mother to convince them of the father's abuse.

If this happens to you as a man, issue an immediate denial and seek a second opinion should your partner bring expert evidence to bear. Check the Expert's credentials first!

Seeking Help

Although men are supposed to be the action orientated doers, even when men are being seriously abused by their partners they have shown reluctance to seek help. The following check list may be useful to you if you feel that you are in a low quality or abusive relationship.

- Does your partner physically attack your genitals when you are defenceless, asleep for example?

- Does your partner use sleep deprivation methods such as sex or arguing late at night or waking you up in the middle of the night?

- Does your partner emasculate you?

- Does your partner ridicule your penis size?

- Does your partner ridicule your sexual performance and compare your performance to past lovers or partners?

- Does your partner coerce you into sex acts against your will?

- Does your partner refuse to have sex or make love unless it is on her terms?

- Does your partner destroy or threaten to destroy personal possessions?

- Does your partner humiliate you in front of other people including your children?

- Does your partner overreact to minor irritations and lose control flying into a rage or tantrum?

- Does your partner consistently lie to you?

- Does your partner criticise you if you spend money on something for yourself?

- Does your partner insult you publicly or at home?

- Does your partner harass you for long periods just to win an argument?

- Does your partner devalue you as a man?

- Does your partner sulk and withdraw affection from you to punish you?

- Does your partner undermine relationships you have with family and friends to isolate you?

- Does your partner threaten self-harm or suicide if you assert your rights or look as though you will end the relationship?

- Does your partner threaten to destroy your relationship with your children?

- Does your partner tell you that no one else would want you as you couldn't cope with a real woman?

- Does your partner threaten to report you to Social Services or the Police as an abusive parent?

- Does your partner tell you that you will never have contact with the children if you end the relationship?

- Does your partner make excessive demands to know where you are and what you are doing and frequently phone you and interrogate you about how you spend your time at work?

- Does your partner tell you that she will make sure that you come out of the divorce with nothing?

- Does your partner impress others with her presentation of self in public but behave differently at home?

- Does your partner threaten to have you thrown out of the home using a court order or lock you out of the home as a punishment?

- Does your partner blame you for her abusive behaviour claiming that it is only you who makes her angry?

If you answer yes to more than 10 of the questions above, you are in an abusive relationship and need help. If you answered yes to more than 5 of the above, then you are in a low quality relationship and are having sexual problems you need help. It is almost impossible to separate psychological and emotional abuse, but all abuse has damaging effects both psychologically and emotionally. What counts as a traumatic life event or abuse is difficult to define but what is well established is that if you experience an event as abusive then it can have an effect on your mental health.

Chapter 3

Domestic Violence and Disharmony Within the Family

'There is no excuse for male violence and too many excuses for female violence' Erin Pizzey

The similarity between my mother and my ex-wife Sophie was confirmed by the various professionals I consulted. It was entirely due to the enormous amount of help from these professionals that enabled me to control and understand the situation I found myself in, particularly Dr Keith Stoll, Dr Malcolm George and Dr Hetty MacKinnon. This chapter is dedicated to those professionals and attempts to give in layman's terms the superb advice I was given.

Subconsciously I had been a victim of domestic violence from my family all my life, as had my sister. I swore that I would never marry anyone who argued continuously as I sat at the top of the stairs aged five hearing my parents screaming at each other. Latterly my brother, Charles, who is smaller than me and very aggressive, conducted a wide ranging campaign of abuse against me from the age of eleven, when he stole my girlfriend of seven years, to the present day. It was only aged 60 that I understood his abusive behaviour, why he did it and its consequences for the whole family.

My mother's abuse was far more direct, she had a fearsome temper and wasn't known as *'World War Three in Knickers'* for nothing! So, from a very early age, I was used to abuse and unwittingly drawn to continue the pattern when I met Sophie in 1996. For a short and happy period, I escaped from the circle of abuse and spent a great deal of the latter part of my youth in Scotland with a family, the Youngers, with whom I was able to find out the meaning of a stable happy family life. When Charles went to work in the Middle East in the 1980s a period of calm and tranquillity reigned at home only to be broken when he returned with his wife in 1985. He did everything in his power to make my life a misery when I divorced and supported Sophie all the way as his wife did. The best move I made was to go back to Scotland in 1996 where Harry and I had a brief but happy time. I have dedicated a bench to him on a tee Gifford Golf Club in East Lothian, now named *'Harry's Rest.'*

The law still allows allegations of violence and sexual abuse to form part of a divorce petition; this fails to protect the abused person and shields the abuser. This is despite the *'No Fault Divorce'* Rules, currently under review, for the umpteenth time. Domestic Violence allegations are one of the few avenues left to obtain Legal Aid. The legal thinking is discussed in detail in Chapter 11 but is based on a system which in the fifties suggested that the man is the cause of all domestic upheaval in a relationship and once removed the violence will cease. What sometimes happens, particularly in the case of women with Personality Disorders, is that the abuser is left with the children. His or her condition is not cured be it alcoholism or depression. With either of these two illnesses the abuser will keep the children at arm's length and push them onto the street where they will rob and steal, money being short and eventually they will end up in prison.

It is commonly known that a number of abusing women, estimated to be 5% of the total, gain custody of their children through violent tactics.

But what is domestic violence and how do we combat it?

We will discuss in this Chapter the problems of violence of men on women and women on men. The problem of domestic violence is on the increase (see Chapter 8) and although it is common to associate the problem with the battered wife the problem of the battered husband also exists. Indeed, in the study carried out for the Met Police by Dr. Malcolm George, he found the ratio of male to female violence was 50:50 not the 70:30 so often rehearsed in Court.

We will divide the Chapter into different segments of domestic violence, physical, emotional and financial.

Physical Violence

Genetic or family dispositions may have drawn you to subconsciously marry an abuser given that men are always seen to be seeking a way back to the womb. Also, you will feel comfortable with the abuse and find it easier to handle. A man or woman who has not experienced a violent childhood will see the symptoms much more clearly than the victim and run away from it. Hence the expression in marriage *'I can't think what she sees in him.'*

Children from families where domestic violence is prevalent will fall into the victim or the abuser role. The *'nature & nurture'* aspects of the upbringing mean that the child with the genetic pre-disposition to aggression will thrive on being an abuser whilst those children without that genetic pre-disposition will become victims to the abuse often throughout their life. Physical violence in a relationship takes many forms.

Expressive Violence

A large number of couples are regarded as tricky or difficult and although the story may be different behind closed doors these are regarded as low grade violent relationships. These will often result in a truce between the two partners and joint agreements that neither should drink at the same time and they should either exercise or have a nanny to *'take the edge'* off the situation. If the couple can either with or without the help of a conciliator find common ground in the relationship (see Chapter 9) the marriage will survive within those boundaries. Holidays and quiet week-ends are often the only remedy needed for this type of relationship where often both couples are working and looking after the children.

This type of violence is known as expressive violence and is defined as violent acts which arise out of the emotional life of the relationship and are not serious or particularly injurious. The role of the aggressor and victim are not fixed in this scenario and so typically one argument between the couple results in either committing an aggressive act. These acts of violence are not intense and seriously injurious and will probably be no more than pushing, shoving or throwing things around.

What is worrying if because of outside factors the marriage becomes untenable the man may be driven to hit due to increased frustration or confusion. Once he hits he is 99% certain to be ousted from the home as the Court will not take into account the factors leading up to that hit.

The frequency of divorces amongst couples who have twins and triplets is another case in point. Triplets mean three times the bottle and feeding times and three times the nappy changing! It is essential in these cases to take advice from such organisations as TAMBA (the Twins and Multiple Birth Association). Help from outside will often relieve the mother of the enormous strain of looking after these children.

Other examples of relationships in this category are a sudden family bereavement or illness, loss of job or moving house. The underlying stress imposed by the above may go unnoticed until it is too late. The main thing to realise is that communication between the two parties is essential and a quick remedy essential either through professionals or self-help. The sudden increase in alcohol consumption or clinical depression caused by an outside event may also happen at a moment's notice. If you find that the problem is unsolvable within the family, you must seek professional help as alcoholism and depression require a course of drugs and/or therapy (see Chapters 5 & 6). As Chapter 3 states, the problems may be social with the two partners having had an elevated idea of the joys of marriage which were satisfactory with money and freedom but without those the relationship regressed into a stayed and boring timetable.

It is essential for both partners, if they wish the relationship to survive to attend all the conciliation and medical courses, dropping out half way can have disastrous consequences.

The Alcoholic or PMS/PND Relationship

Alcohol and PMS are common factors in a number of relationship breakdowns but it the associated problems that go with the alcoholic or the PMS sufferer which can destroy the relationship. The couple have married on a cloud and settled into married routine with the husband being the bread winner and the wife the housewife. Parties are often the norm with both parties drinking to excess and the odd row occurring. When this relationship goes out of kilter with the husband or wife suddenly drinking more or the wife's PMS problems becoming more noticeable either party must take action the sufferer may well be in denial and blaming his or her increased state on his or her partner or the children without looking at himself or herself. They may not see the damage being done to the relationship as in previous relationship's the other partner may have put up with the associated abuse from alcohol or PMS.

If the violence has started after the birth of a child, your wife may be suffering from Post Natal Depression (PND). Although called Post Natal Depression this illness can take a number of facets (see Chapter 4) and if not combated early can lead to other complication following the commencement of menstruation. This type of violence is very frightening as the person concerned has suffered a complete character change leaving the husband and the sufferer very confused.

If you are the husband of a PMS sufferer or the wife of an alcoholic and are experiencing violence, which is in itself upsetting to the children, seek immediate help.

The sufferer may still love you dearly but finds it quite impossible to express his or her feelings either due to the denial factor or the fact that they might be taken off to a psychiatric hospital.

Personality Disorders, Epilepsy, Brain Tumours and Episodic Dyscontrol Syndrome (EDS)

The above behaviour disorders cause the most problems for physicians trying to help problems in a relationship especially the former which, being a disorder of the persona is virtually impossible to treat.

One of the main factors in deciding the root of the problem is the remorse and trigger factors. If your partner remembers the violent outburst and is sorry for the act, the possibility is that the problem is epileptic related or EDS. If your partner has a sudden outburst of anger which is frightening and comes out of the blue and causes distress and does not have any remorse, there is a possibility of Personality Disorder or brain tumour. One way of finding out the root cause of the problem is for the GP to refer the patient for an Electroencephalographic (EEG) analysis. The result of this analysis will either show a clear reading or problems associated with the brain. The patient's attack may have been so severe that he or she may not have any idea of the attack or what he or she did during the attack that the EEG is the *'fingerprint'* to the problem. If the first EEG shows a problem, a subsequent sleep induced EEG may pinpoint the problem. If the problem still exists it is often necessary to have a brain scan to check for the presence of a tumour.

The EEG will also determine whether the problem is epileptic, EDS, a brain tumour or personality disorder; if it is the latter the final diagnosis rests with the behaviour of the individual. In addition, if he or she cannot see a reason not to behave in that manner and the triggers are trivial, more likely or not the problem is one of Personality Disorder.

Epileptic attacks are usually random occurring at any time or place. If the EEG or brain scan reading is on the left hand temporal lobe there are a number of behavioural problems associated with damage to the left hand temporal lobe. Temporal lobe epilepsy is the commonest form of epilepsy in man. Scarring is the commonest cause of temporal lobe epilepsy from head injury or infection such as whooping cough. The temporal lobes are the commonest places for small mal-formations to occur. The left hand temporal lobe has more emphasis on intellectual function, particularly speech. (Dr T.A. Betts)

Some research suggests that in the case of personality disordered people that part of the brain is immature and late in developing thus the sufferer will exhibit tendencies of the *'spoilt little child.'* Treatment is possible for sufferers of EDS and epilepsy; a course of epileptic drugs may be administered with the advice to lay off alcohol. It may be noticed in cases where the woman is the sufferer that her disorder gets worse during her menstruation, under stress or after heavy alcohol consumption, as alcohol is a catalyst for oestrogen, which tumours such as meningiomas feed on. The control or awareness of these factors should limit the damage.

As already stated, the treatment of EDS or epilepsy is possible with sometimes a lobotomy being performed on the patient. Personality disorder has such terrible side effects that its treatment is known as the psychiatrist's nightmare and specialists are very wary in diagnosing the problem given there is no cure. As it is borderline the probability of making the wrong diagnosis is very common where children are involved, and it is usually the recommendation of a specialist who suspects a personality disorder for the matter to be ultimately heard in Court and obtain the disparate versions from both parties. Although there is no law in place at the moment, it is hoped with the current divorce changes that female or male sufferers of personality disorder whose children are at risk will lose custody of the children if they refuse treatment. One key part of the process I campaigned for was the use of scans as evidence in Court.

The Characteristics of Personality Disorders

Personality Disorder is a term which has recently hit the headlines as a mental condition which may lead an individual to commit serious criminal acts. Like most medical terms, few outside medicine, and in this case the related fields of psychology, would know what such a condition is or what might be the attributes of an individual which might lead to such a diagnosis. The Family Division appears oblivious of the condition and its effects on the family.

At its simplest level the person with such a disorder has a personality which is at the very limits of what are considered the normal range. He is not psychotic and does not totally lack the insight into his behaviour as the psychotic does.

The Diagnostic and Statistical Manual of the American Psychiatric Association (DSM-IIIR) defines such disorders as a category of disorders which are distinct from affective disorders such as depression and schizophrenia. The individual with a personality disorder has a maladaptive behaviour pattern which is persistent over time and involves a disruption of social relationships. The individual does not suffer in the sense that the depressive or schizophrenic does; but his family, friends and society do suffer the consequences of his or her maladaptive behaviour.

He or she is distinguished from the normal population by a lack of complete insight into his behaviour, repeating socially unacceptable behaviour seemingly without regard to the suffering it causes others. Characteristically he or she denies fault and always attributes blame to others; society is to blame for his problems and never himself.

Personality disorders arise from genetic predispositions and from *'faulty'* upbringing and persist throughout life, although they may be less overt from middle age onwards. In some instances, they may arise from damage to the brain during adulthood or birth, but essentially diagnosis usually relies on a history of maladaptive behaviour from childhood or adolescence onwards. A crucial factor which differentiates these disorders from other affective disorders is an absence of ideation hallucination or delusion.

There are many different types of Personality Disorder of which the most widely known is the sociopath, or as most would call it psychopath. The psychopath is a bully who enjoys his own perception of himself as strong and others as weak. He or she is immune to the suffering of others and has shallow affection towards others. Frequently this type of personality engages in criminal activity and will use the violence with little provocation. Whilst poor work and marital records often occur it is important to note that many psychopaths are able, if they find work in which their quest for dominance can be fulfilled, to sustain successful employment. Like other personality disorder types, the psychopath can be charming and popular but will tend to be unable to sustain social relations over time. His attraction to others allows the psychopath to *'use'* his victims to satisfy his demands until they find him too excessive to reject him.

Psychopathy is characteristic of many male and female batterers, indeed some forms of personality disorder are three times more common in women than men. The popular image of the cold killer is true in the most extreme cases, but it should be noted that this disorder is more common than those cases of cold calculating murders.

The Borderline or Histrionic Personality is perhaps the female equivalent of the male psychopath and often psychopathic behaviour is part of this disorder. Borderline personalities are quick to anger and are exceedingly demanding and attention seeking. Impulsivity and drama and the need to be the centre of attention are characteristics and violence is often a part of this individual's behaviour patterns. In contrast to the psychopath which because of the known association with criminality is well studied, the Borderline Personality has been less well studied. One of the characteristics of this personality is the propensity to self-injury or illness feigning (Munchausen's syndrome) as a means of attracting attention. As with the psychopath affection is insincere and shallow and both are manipulative of others to their own ends. Marital record of such individuals is poor and sexual behaviour may vary from frigidity to promiscuity but is rarely functional and satisfying. Together with the psychopath abuse of alcohol or drugs is often a complicating factor. In both these disorders a lack of remorse for their offences against others is another characteristic.

The incidence of the Borderline Personality is unknown, but it is thought to be quite common among the female population.

One of the great problems associated with the individual with a personality disorder is that he or she believes there is nothing wrong with him or her. After all he has an unshakeable belief that it is others that are the problem and so he or she rarely seeks medical help. It is his or her family and friends that suffer and it is often they that attempt to initiate medical intervention.

Other disorders than the Borderline and Psychopath are also defined but such individuals are less of a problem for others.

Personality disorders are notoriously difficult to treat and often such individuals are some of the most difficult and disruptive patients within mental institutions. Some success has been reported with prolonged group psychotherapy, but often this is only possible within prisons or secure mental institutions where there is an element of compulsion to treatment.

Outside such a setting, because the individual does not see he has a problem, any attempted treatment is often terminated by the individual. Some success is beginning to be achieved with drug treatments as understanding of the brain function and its disruption in psychiatric illness is becoming better understood.

Childhood conduct disorders, family breakdown, child abuse and neglect and family history of such disorder are all factors predictive of children growing into adulthood with such personality problems.

In the diagnosis of psychiatric disease, it is sometimes the case that personality disorder diagnoses are accompanied by disorders of affect e.g. psychosis, depression etc.

It is easy to miss apply the term Personality Disorder and diagnosis can only be made by professionals against a set list of diagnostic criteria such as described above.

For a very lucid and readily readable account of the whole subject of personality disorders consult *Personality Disorders In Principles of Abnormal Psychology,* Chapter 13, by H. Munsinger, published by Macmillan 1983.

Psychological Instrumental Violence

Where there is no evidence of a structural disorder in the brain the probable reason for the violence will be the controlling partner exerting his or her control in any manner possible. Instrumental violence is more problematic, potentially much more injurious and the role of the victim and abuser are fixed. It is called instrumental violence because it is a goal directed i.e. to control or punish. Typically, in this relationship other abusive behaviours will also be used. Total verbal derogation of the victim to destroy self-confidence are accompanied by fear provoking threats. The on-going and unremitting process of emotional and psychological bullying may be accompanied by such features as jealousy, alcohol abuse, (see Chapter 5) financial abuse and, most distressingly, sexual abuse and abuse of the couple's children. In this type of domestic abuse, the violence is merely the backdrop to the enforcement of the all-embracing system of emotional and psychological torture aimed at total domination and control. When violence is used it can be mercilessly vicious and severe.

The victim is usually isolated by the abuser from the supportive contact of family and friends and experiences a sense of great fear, helplessness and hopelessness which prevents them from escaping from the relationship. Physical flight may be even more difficult given the necessities of obtaining alternative accommodation, financial worries and concerns for the children. It is invariably the case that the instrumental abuser will be popular with others and seem charming in public life, only showing the full panoply of abusive behaviours *'behind closed doors.'* They may have important jobs or prestigious careers and have a respectability amongst their friends, work colleagues and community that belies their behaviour inside the home. This, of course, is the way they found their domestic victim in the first place - they seemed to be wonderful outgoing, social and charming people.

This is the form of domestic abuse seen in the worst cases of wife abuse and portrayed in graphic and moving accounts of battered wives. It is this form of domestic abuse that the term *'battering'* is more correctly applied. It has become fashionable in this case to talk of the *'cycle of violence'* (see fig 1) in which a circle of tension and abusive events leads up to a violent episode, which is followed by the abuser being sorrowful for their actions and promising never to repeat them. Unfortunately, such promises are made to be broken, for in themselves they are part of the game of psychological terror the abuser is exercising on the victim; in reality such remorse is a sham.

In some individuals it has been learnt from childhood that aggression and violence are rewarding and allow the individual to satisfy impulses and obtain gratification not attainable by other means. In this instance the individual is unlikely to see aggression and violence as wrong and feel troubled by using it. There is a lack of the normal behaviour inhibition to such anti-social behaviour. This is the picture of the individual who may well be habitually and criminally violent and also be the worst kind of spouse abuser. More often, however, a violent act by most individuals is essentially a fear response. When the environment presents us with threats which we see as challenging to our integrity either physically of to our concept of ourselves as an individual our brains can direct us to respond to the threat by using what is called the *'Fight or Flight'* response.

Fig. 1: DOMESTIC ABUSE INTERVENTION PROJECT
206 West Fourth Street
Duluth, Minnesota 55806
218-722-1134

Financial abuse is very common in Upper/Middle Class English and Asian families. The husband or wife will hold onto the purse strings and only give out money in extreme circumstances. This enables the abuser to maintain total control of the victim be it his wife or children. Money will often be lavishly spent on such items as medical bills or legal fees which provide little or no enjoyment for the family.

The abuser may be deeply unhappy in his or her self and seeing that his or her family are enjoying themselves and he or she cannot, situations are created where that enjoyment ceases. Family occasions can reach a certain level of fun but after a time the control returns and the party falls flat.

In the opposite direction, the use of almost any violent act by a man's female partner is seen as a legitimate act of self-defence following provocation. The 1990's ruling in the High Court regarding the matter of provocation in the Emma Humphreys case, whilst perfectly reasonable in that context, should be viewed with caution in other cases, as the use of the *'provocation rule'* will protect violent women and men who murder and could kill again because of the presence of personality disorder. The beliefs concerning *'self-defence,'* of course are based firmly on the basis of assumptions. There are a great many couples suffering worst cases of abuse than in these cases and they never resort to a homicide.

There is however another way of looking at the situation, some women are violent. Some men who experience violence from a female just do not believe that it is acceptable behaviour to hit a woman, not even to retaliate - *'take it like a man'* - in a number of cases the man will only seek help when the violence is directed at the children and the man is worried for their safety. In cases of severe PND the mother may kill or attempt to kill the child and cover up the problem as cot death. The reality of the problem is that some women do kill their children before the age of 1 year old. There were 300 unsolved murders of children under 1in 1994. If the mother fails to kill her child before 1 year old the next tactic is to put that child in a situation where he or she can kill themselves in such accidents as drowning or traffic accident. The mother will then become the grieving mother at the funeral and receive undivided attention and concern. The figures of child abuse bear this problem out and although it is well known to exist – the authorities cover the problem up by fair means or foul and will usually act in the wrong circumstances or when it is too late.

Most men will let their partners get away with an occasional slap and indeed many men interviewed regarded it as the norm. To quote David Thomas from his book *Not Guilty in the Defence of Modern Man, 'equality is not a buffet; you cannot pick and choose.'*

At the end of the day the secret of remaining in an abusive relationship is to understand the problem and then tackle it. As a man you will have enormous amount of dirt thrown at you by your wife and the authorities.

But don't forget a custody case is never over and you can fight until the sea freezes over.

The problem of female violence is already recognised in the United States and Courts have been established to help the abused and the abuser.

Whether you are male of female you owe it to your children to come to rational solution.

Case Study

A little boy aged six pleaded with his dad not to take him home as *'they would do it again.'* The Social Services said to the father that they would wait six months before taking action. The little boy was being buggered by his step-father with the mother looking on.

Case Study – Geoffrey

After the wedding she was fine until they had to move house when she became very difficult but once moved in was fine. Their daughter was conceived and at the start of pregnancy she was very difficult and aggressive, demanding extra money, being very hyper active and bad tempered.

The aggression and odd behaviour continued until Geoffrey consulted her private GP. By this time Geoffrey had been attacked and his wife had broken all the glasses in their flat. Their daughter was nervous of her mother.

The behaviour continued and he consulted a psychologist. The psychologist was not hopeful and put it down to her family problems and advised against having more children as should it be a girl the wife would treat the girl as she had been treated by her mother. The psychologist saw the wife and told Geoffrey that there was nothing he could do, she was a *'chameleon'* and did not see the need for help. Geoffrey should not confront her and if she became aggressive he should leave the house.

Nothing changed and Geoffrey went back for help and the psychiatrist agreed to see them both. The next day the psychiatrist wanted a second opinion and suggested a neurologist.

On their return she announced that she was leaving him and that if he didn't go she would get him out. Geoffrey went to the solicitor and an injunction was served to stop her leaving the country as well as the divorce papers. She retaliated with an Ouster Application making false allegations against Geoffrey which were left undefended by his lawyers.

Three weeks later Geoffrey's wife attacked him when he was changing his daughter's nappy. He pushed her away and called the Police. When the Police arrived, she had calmed down and no action was taken. Her solicitor reinstated the Ouster Application and despite Geoffrey's protestations that he was innocent he was advised to leave. His ex-wife murdered their daughter fifteen years later

Case Study – Trevor

Trevor met his wife who was Scandinavian at an airport. They were happily married with one child when Trevor came back to the flat to find that she had totally destroyed it with the child present. He took her to hospital where she was prescribed some tranquillisers. She then smashed up the flat again and Trevor went for custody of his child. After a twelve day hearing the judge came down on the mother's side because she was being prescribed medication to prevent her losing control.

It is a known fact that women with this condition are not totally safe with their children when the three factors of alcohol, stress and her period come into play is neither here nor there. Trevor lost custody at a cost of £109,000; his ex-wife committed suicide one year later.

Case Study - Francis

Francis was married with a six year old son when the attacks began. He had suffered various attacks before, but the violence increased suddenly and he was attacked several times resulting in a broken nose, a broken arm, cuts and bruises and finally he was attacked by a spanner and knocked on the head.

He admitted to me that on the occasion his nose was broken he did hit his wife in self-defence. On one occasion his son had a black eye where he had tried to defend his grandmother from attack by his mother. Francis was ousted from the house and he lost everything apart from a trumpet. He pays his wife £8,000 per year and has not seen his son for eight years. On one visit he heard a loud crack behind his head and his ex-wife had attempted to hit him with a billiard cue, luckily for him the cue contacted with the door lintel.

Case Study – Max

Max is a professional man and the attacks first started when his wife began to demand more sex. She would bar the door and grab Max's testicles and squeeze them until he gave in. On other occasions she would hit him with objects such as hammers and throw sharp glass ash trays at him. The Police have been called many times and have done nothing. It is recognised that his wife is suffering from a personality disorder, but the authorities will do nothing about it. His wife took their daughter to Greece and he never saw her again.

Chapter 4

Post Natal Depression and Pre Menstrual Tension The Effect on the Marriage

Wendy Holton, PMS Help

'The presence of symptoms in the days before menstruation with complete absence of symptoms after menstruation'
The definition of pre-menstrual syndrome, or PMS

It is well known that *'illness'* of one kind or another can often be an important cause for the break-up of a relationship, the *'illness'* is always imagined to be of some serious nature with the patient being confined to bed for some considerable period of time. There is always a great deal of sympathy and concern for the patient, often the other partner is seen to be running away from the situation and less consideration is shown to them in these circumstances.

If this illness rarely confines the sufferer to bed, or at least not for a continuous time, he or she is not seen as ill but as being awkward or constantly changing and thus deserving of no sympathy, but ridicule or even contempt. If the pattern of illness described above is persistent and the sufferer is female, she may in fact be suffering from pre-menstrual syndrome (PMS) with hormonal fluctuations causing the changes.

The symptoms of PMS are many and varied, they can be those of tension, depression or lethargy we read about in the media. They can also include the physical symptoms of backache, headaches, sore breasts or bloatedness (when there may or may not be an actual weight gain). They could also include asthma, spotty skin, a feeling of worthlessness, aggressive outbursts or even violence to another person, themselves or their surroundings.

There have been over 150 different symptoms of PMS reported in medical literature. The main criteria is for these symptoms to recur before menstruation and to disappear when the full menstrual flow occurs.

The pre-menstrual syndrome may have started with puberty or later, a very common time being after pregnancy. Some women find that it may start after a subsequent pregnancy. It could also start on stopping the oral contraceptive pill, after a miscarriage or termination or even after sterilisation. These are all times of hormonal upheaval and are the major triggers for PMS and PND to start or to increase in severity. Your partner may have had quite mild PMS when you first met, after the first childbirth it got worse but perhaps after the second pregnancy the PMS reached a point where it was actually destroying the happy family you had both planned and worked so hard for.

There is also a very strong link between post-natal depression (PND) and the more severe condition puerperal psychosis, and PMS. In fact, some 80% of women who suffer from PND go on to experience PMS. It was in France in the late 1850's that the physician Maree noted that in his patients with PND, improvement came after menstruation with the symptoms returning with greater severity before the next menstruation. When they were well this was always after menstruation with a return of the horrific symptoms before the onset of the next menstrual flow. It is not always appreciated that the symptoms of PND, sometimes more correctly referred to as post-natal illness, do not necessarily include depression or the usual symptoms of depression.

The commonest first symptoms reported tend to be Anxiety, Tiredness, Insomnia, Confusion, Irritability, Agitation and Hyperactivity before the patient reports *'depression'* as a symptom to the GP. Thus, if your partner has recently given birth and she is exhibiting any of the above symptoms, consider carefully the possibility that she has PND, for this may be a cause of her problems.

Seek professional help for her, don't abandon her or the child. The first step is to ensure that she is eating the 3 hourly starchy diet, even if it means waking when she feeds the baby and having half a sandwich or a couple of crispbreads with her. Also remember to tell the GP and gynaecologist about these problems before the next baby as there are now ways of combating the problem before delivery of the child.

Many women find that their PMS is worse when on the oral contraceptive pill, although doctors continue to prescribe this. Unfortunately, all forms of oral contraceptive pill contain progestogens which are synthetic hormones alien to the human body, and these lower the progesterone level. If when taking the pill your partner finds that she has side effects, she should give serious consideration to trying another form of contraception. Alas sterilisation will often make PMS worse, as by blocking the tubes in whatever way it is done causes hormonal upset and imbalance. Thus, women who suffer severe PMS will have to consider other forms of contraception, either an intrauterine device, often referred to as *'the coil'* or a barrier method of contraception such as the cap, sheath, female condom or even a vasectomy for her partner.

The symptoms come and go and are cyclical in nature but when present can be very severe and may even cause a character change. The partner may also find it very difficult explaining the *'illness'* to the GP as often when either he or his partner decide to visit the GP the symptoms have gone and there are no visible signs of the symptoms described.

At certain times you will find that you can do nothing right. If you bring home chocolates you are shouted at because she is trying to diet, if you bring roses home she will accuse you of buying them for a girlfriend, if you come home early you are spying on her but if you are 5 minutes late you are accused of abandoning her, whatever the situation you cannot win. You must understand that she is helpless in controlling these character changes which are sudden and inexplicable and leave the sufferer helpless in trying to explain and handle this Jekyll and Hyde change.

Who can blame the man who after many years of this behaviour takes the advice of his partner and gets out of her life. It is very common for women with this problem to blame their partner for the problem as they are often in a period of denial. The departure of the male partner may relieve the tensions for a short time but two weeks later she may be begging you to return promising that the problem will not recur. In situations where as a last resort the man may have consulted a lawyer the chances of retrieving the marriage by explaining to the lawyer that PMS was the cause may be too late as the process of separation may well have started.

If as a man you are in the situation where your partner has these symptoms and asks you to leave, don't try and solve the problem at home with professional help. There is a possibility that due to the disruption and uncertainty caused she too may have consulted a lawyer, and once you have left getting back is almost impossible if lawyers are involved. Often the man will take a short term measure and leave the house to go to friends or the pub to defuse the immediate situation coming back late when his partner is asleep. Here again he may find a sympathetic female ear or bottle either of which will cause more problems than they solve. If you have small children make sure that they are being looked after properly during this period and explain to them the problem if they are old enough. Try and avoid any yo-yo situation where the problems come and go with the symptoms, seek help quickly. To enable the problem to be solved for the whole family the sufferer must be able to understand the situation herself. The definition of pre-menstrual syndrome, or PMS is, *'The presence of symptoms in the days before menstruation with complete absence of symptoms after menstruation.'* This is a very simple and definite definition. The symptoms can be present for up to 14 days before menstruation, but after the menstrual flow there is at least 7 days without the symptoms, whatever they may be.

There is a great deal that can be done to help the situation. The first is to appreciate that your partner would love to be relieved of this changing character and that although you may think that she is doing it to attract attention often she does in fact try very hard not to be two different characters, she would rather be welcoming and loving all the time. However, her actions are caused by the changing hormonal levels during the menstrual cycle.

The simple way to track the problem is to mark on a chart (see Fig. 1) a symbol depicting the presence of the symptoms, it may be 'A' for argumentative, 'V' for vixen-like of 'L' for lethargic and doesn't feel like going out or doing the house work.

After a couple of months you will see if there is a pattern emerging with the symptoms occurring in the days before menstruation and absent afterwards.

If the pattern is definite then your partner is likely to be suffering from PMS and needs help. It is advisable for you not to confront her with the chart during her pre-menstrual phase, wait until she is her *'well'* state when you can sit down, look at the chart and discuss the situation. Should you both decide to seek help from a doctor, take the chart with you, making sure that again the appointment is made when she is in her 'well' state.

It is often found that following this visit and the problem is solved and a lot of the uncertainty over the possible causes of the *'illness'* be it brain tumour or depression have been discounted your partner will feel far happier in herself which will reflect on her behaviour within the family.

The spectre of mental illness haunts both men and women and for GPs not understanding PMS the first diagnosis will often be depression and a course of anti-depressants.

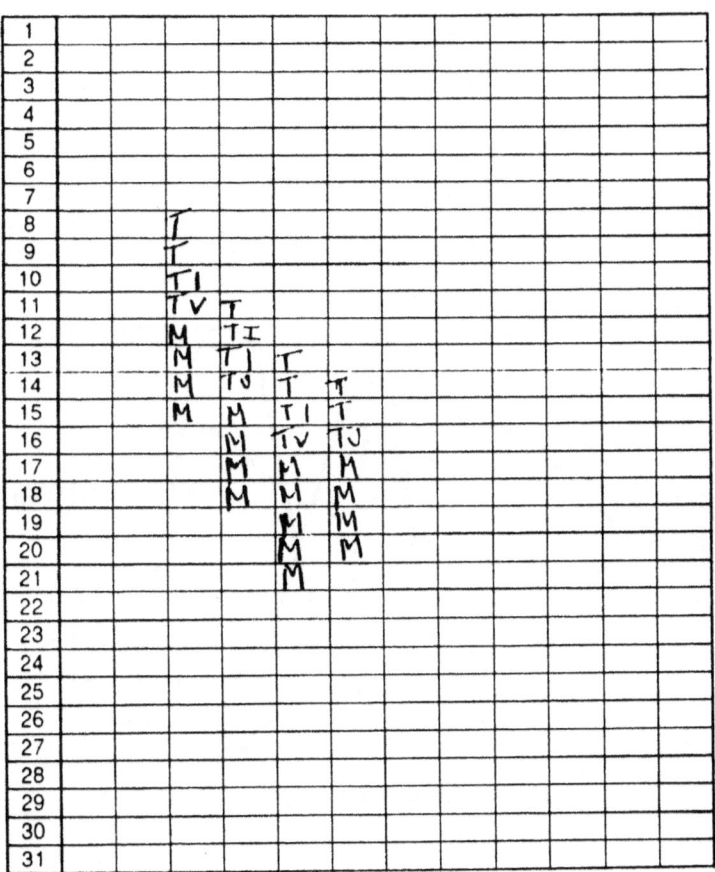

Fig. 1: Menstrual Chart showing PMS

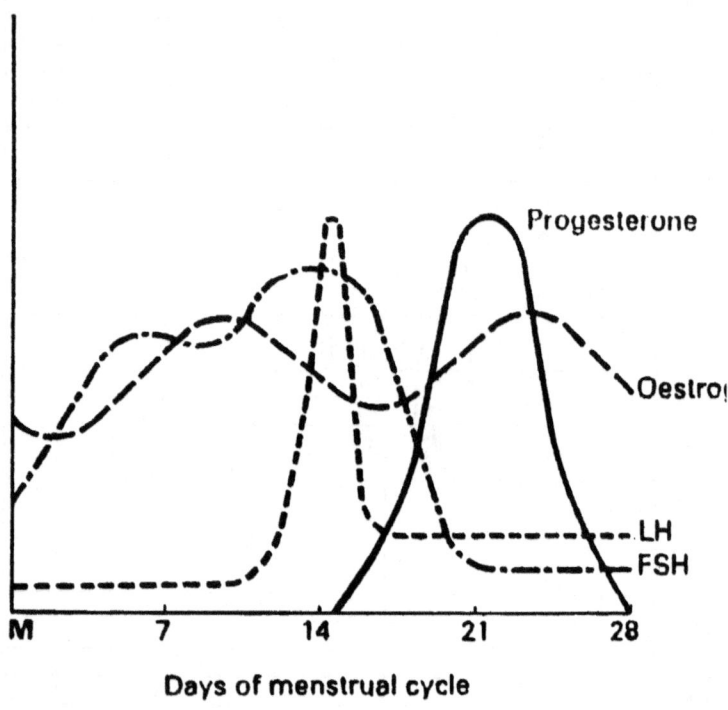

Fig 2: Levels of Progesterone, Oestrogen, LH and FSH

If the chart pattern is not definite it might be worth continuing charting the presence of symptoms and see if you can find the pattern or root cause of the outbursts. It may be that the problems always occur at weekends when the routine is interrupted and the family are making considerable demands on her time and energy. It is possible that she may behaving long food gaps at weekends and this drop in blood sugar is part of the root cause.

It may be that the symptoms occur on particular days of the week or are just randomly spread throughout the week or month. In either case when she is in a position to discuss the situation then you should show her the chart and see if a solution can be found.

In Fig 2 you will see the four hormones involved in the female reproductive cycle and that at each day they are at a different ratio to one another. This difference occurs whatever the length of your partner's menstrual cycle, whether she has a 21 day cycle or one of 38 days or more, there are never two days with the identical ratio of hormones. When you realise that this fluctuation occurs throughout the menstrual cycle from puberty (average age13) until the menopause (average 51 years) you will probably appreciate why these ratios go haywire in certain women.

It must also be appreciated that progesterone and oestrogen as well as being hormones involved in reproduction, also have many other functions within the human body. One of the functions of the hormone progesterone is glucose metabolism; it is this function which is so often the key to helping sufferers of PMS. Throughout the body there are progesterone receptors whose task is to transport molecules of progesterone to the cell nucleus where it is needed.

They cannot do this when there has been a drop in blood sugar level as their function is maintaining glucose metabolism is then required. Because of the many functions of progesterone there are numerous progesterone receptor sites in the brain, in the meninges surrounding the brain, in the bones, in the nasopharyngeal passages, eyes, liver, breasts and of course in the genital area.

Thus, a simple and very effective first step in helping a PMS sufferer is to ensure that the blood sugar level is maintained at a steady level all through the day, throughout the month. In fact this rule applies equally to anyone else who suffers from sudden outbursts of argumentative or destructive behaviour, regardless of sex or age. But how is this balance achieved?

You need to ensure that your partner has small portions of starchy food, every three hours of her waking day; within one hour of waking and on hour of retiring to bed at night, every day of the month. The starchy foods are those containing flour, rice, oats, potatoes, maize and rye.

These simple and stable foods are needed in quite small amounts, and contrary to opinion in the 1950s, they are not fattening. In fact they are some of the low calorie foods and will only encourage good health in the eater. The emphasis is only on small portions and what is suggested is to divide the daily food intake into six or seven snacks each containing some starch.

Thus, if your partner has cereal for breakfast, have a smaller portion and a crispbread, a slice of bread or toast or possibly 2 biscuits mid morning. Instead of a sandwich, fruit and yoghurt at lunch, eat only half the sandwich and have the other half 3 hours later. Again, keep some part of the supper back and have it before bed so that the total calorie intake is the same but spread evenly over the day. If there is no time for breakfast because of getting the children ready for school encourage your partner to have something even if it is only a slice of toast or bread as soon as she wakes, this will be quite sufficient to keep the blood sugar level even until mid-morning if she then has some further starch. You will see the change this small measure will make as about 45% of PMS sufferers skip breakfast.

To maintain good health this diet rule needs to be combined with at least two portions of protein, the main sources being: fish, meat, eggs, cheeses or pulses and some fresh fruit or vegetables each day.

In fact, the starchy food at 3 hourly intervals, or less, will encourage lower cholesterol levels. It will also stop those binges which are so common when she will suddenly eat a whole box of chocolates, or two chocolate bars without stopping.

Your partner will need to be encouraged in this new eating habit, if the children are of school age and can count, they should have the simple rules explained to them; they are wonderful at ensuring that Mum eats regularly if it means they can have some too. It is also beneficial for men to maintain a steady blood sugar level so the whole family can join in the process. The crumbs in the bed after the biscuit eaten in the early morning are more than a compensation for an even tempered partner.

A drop in blood sugar level will cause a spurt of adrenalin to help the body obtain the stored sugar to raise the blood sugar level again. Adrenalin is the hormone of fight, fright and flight, so often it is the surge of adrenalin which is present when the sufferer suddenly screams, throws or hits out at whatever happens to be present, unfortunately often their nearest and dearest. The symptoms of hyperactivity are caused by frequent adrenalin surges.

Research has shown that these simple steps will ease, if not totally relieve the symptoms of up to 89% of sufferers and over one-third of severe sufferers will get total relief by eating small portions of starchy food every 3 hours of their day throughout the month, many husbands have commented that having tried this eating regime their partner returns to *'being the girl I married.'*

In 1989 severe PMS sufferers who had been referred to a PMS Clinic in London were asked to detail all they ate during 7 consecutive days prior to their appointment. The results showed that 97% had long food gaps during the day and 75% went over 14 hours overnight without any starch containing foods. They were advised to stick rigidly to the 3 hourly starch diet as detailed and within two months 90% had a greater reduction in symptoms, 64% found that their symptoms were relieved or at an acceptable level. Less than one third of these severe sufferers required no further treatment than the reminder of a good diet containing regular starchy snacks every 3 hours of the waking day.

Following the above programme which does not involve psychiatrists, lawyers or drugs but straightforward sound eating is a small step to take to save your relationship and your children's future stability and happiness. The main advice is to grasp the situation as soon as it arises, don't let it fester within the relationship.

Chapter 5

Addiction - The Family Solution

The Chemical Dependency Centre

In this chapter we will deal with drug and alcohol problem in families, its effect on the family and the treatment provided by such organisations as The Chemical Dependency Centre.

Addiction to drugs and alcohol can manifest itself in a number of ways and the resulting harm to the addict and his family is often irreparable. If the spouse or children of the addict can spot the tell-tale signs at an early period of the addiction and seek help, there is a good chance that the addict can be helped and the family unit kept intact. Old forms of treatment for addiction usually resulted in the immediate family being excluded from the process and as the addict emerged from recovery the family were in such a state of confusion that inevitably the marriage failed and the family were split up leaving the addict exposed to a recurrence of his or her problem. The other spouse having had no counselling explaining the reasons for his attachment to the person will invariably fall into the same trap again and marry another addict. Children of addicts are the most exposed to the problem and they will invariably become addicts or marry addicts in later life. The damage done by an uncontrolled addict in a family is catastrophic and if left for long periods can result in the breakup of the whole family unit.

The law has failed to recognise the problem of addicts in marriage and has no mechanism to deal with the problem within the marriage especially when the addict is female.

If the addict is male it is common for the woman to be advised to divorce if the problem is too great; this leaves the male very exposed, lonely and broke and usually leads to death by suicide, overdose or ciahrossis later on.

If the female is an addict and is left with the children she continues to drink or take drugs, spends all the maintenance money on drink or drugs and screams at the husband for money when he turns up for his access visit. The law often decides that it must be the husband who is the cause of the disruption and bans him from seeing his children for a long period. The woman continues to drink or take drugs, money becomes very short and the children are put onto the streets to beg for food or steal. This is the start of juvenile delinquency which often results in the child being sent to prison or put into a home.

Before this draconian process is put into play we must have a process whereby an addict can be helped at an early stage in his or her addiction and the whole family counselled on how to deal with the problem.

The longer the problem is left the more devious the addict becomes and the more the strain shows on the family. By and large the male addict especially in the case of alcoholics is easier to spot as he has *'watering holes'* that can be pinpointed and his friends will begin to take notice and talk to the spouse. He may be drinking at the office or on his way home and invariably be stopped for drinking and driving. The female alcoholic/drug addict is a different problem as by and large she will use her habit alone at home after the children have gone to school or at work. Caterers number among the top echelon of female addicts, a profession where their addiction can easily be covered up by their work in the kitchen.

In the kitchen there is a ready source of alcohol and its presence is very tempting for the addict. Also, caterers work long hours in the evening and it is quite acceptable in many families for the working cook to come back late a little *'tired and emotional'* after a long working evening.

The whole process of spotting the addiction can be complicated by the fact that both partners are drinking, the denial factor, cross addiction to sleeping pills, and transference of the problem to the other spouse.

For the recovery process to work properly the life style and habits of the man must be examined to check that he hasn't got another addiction such as gambling or is a workaholic or he is beating or abusing his wife causing the addiction.

In many cases the addict will have been brought up in an alcoholic environment and will therefore not notice the addiction as he or she is used to living in that environment. It is often the arrival of a child which exposes the addiction as young children are very demanding and often cause the start of the addiction in the mother due to stress factors and tiredness. The signs of addiction take many forms depending on the type of addiction and the individual concerned. Many people deny that they have a problem with alcohol or drugs they often latch on to an outside factor affecting their lives such as family upheaval or job loss as the blame factor.

Denial of the fact can cause the addict to lie, cheat and steal to obtain the relief of alcohol or drugs.

The addict will often have to reach rock bottom before he or she will admit to the addiction, often this is too late and the damage done is terminal or semi-permanent.

Early signs are loss of self-esteem, tiredness, irritability and mood swings. Once the spouse sees a pattern emerging he or she must do something immediately as that pattern will then establish itself into a permanent problem which leads to health problems in the form of liver or kidney failure, not eating, psychological problems, mood swings and lack of sleep.

Beware, the alcoholic or addict is not spotted because he or she is swaying around slurring their words, the true alcoholic can hide their addiction and only start swaying around when they have gone over her very strict schedule of drinking. Alcohol is a very rich food in terms of calories, one ounce of pure alcohol contains about 170 calories when broken down. Continued abuse of alcohol may result in the addict's body rejecting other food thus weight loss & undereating occurs. The immediate fix from the first shot of alcohol or drugs will have an immediate effect on the brain cells as they can easily absorb the substances. The person will become exuberant, chatty and active, very often dancing or talking well into the night. If they are a true alcoholic the first signs will be a bad hangover in the morning, not wanting to get up and consuming large amounts of coffee and cigarettes. In the latter stages this turns into a vodka and orange for breakfast to counteract the terrible withdrawal symptoms. Here we must remember that an alcoholic is not an alcoholic because they drink too much, an alcoholic may drink very little but their character can change dramatically from the effect of the alcohol. It is a well-documented fact that a woman starting her period will become drunk a lot quicker due to her body retaining fluid more readily.

Heavy drinkers can control their bodies up to a point, but the true alcoholic cannot control the damage to their systems and families and without treatment will invariably end up with a broken marriage, in hospital or prison or dead from the addiction.

To give an idea as to the size of the problem over 100 million people in the USA drink alcohol of which 10 million are alcoholics. There are no comparable statistics in the UK, but a survey in the 1990s suggested that 30% of the population regularly consume over the suggested weekly limit of 21 units for a man and 14 for a woman.

The Chemical Dependency Centre & the Radcliffe Project

In the next part of the chapter we describe the operations of the Chemical Dependency Centre & the Radcliffe Project as an example of a specialist addiction clinic. Be warned to choose the right clinic or doctor who should be approved by the NHS or BUPA as the wrong clinic or doctor can cause permanent damage to the addict and his or her family. Dr Dalton's PMS Help in Chapter 4 has great experience in dealing with women with addiction problems and can help in the initial treatment of PMS and alcohol and drugs problems.

The Chemical Dependency Centre (CDC) was started by Tristan Millington-Drake after a traumatic time in helping his father through an addiction to alcohol which eventually led to his early death. The Centre is now so well established and respected that Health & Local Authorities purchase its services in helping addiction recovery; your GP will be able to refer you to the Centre. The Centre, based in Earl's Court is divided into three units, the two homes, Thurston House, a 23 bed residential secondary Home for men recovering from drug and alcohol dependency, Hope House an 8 bed secondary care home for women recovering from alcohol or drug dependency, the Redcliffe Project which provides a screening service and SHARP providing a primary day care service and aftercare for recovering addicts and their families.

The importance of involving the whole family at a very early stage in the process is vital for the success of the treatment. The Centre recommends the same treatment for both alcohol and drug addiction problems as it is now recognised that users of alcohol & drugs in the main abuse both substances when their addiction has got out of control.

If the addict requires detoxification at a time when the drug has taken over his or her body and it cannot function without the drugs, then The Centre will arrange for the patient to be sent to a specialist unit. Detoxification is a very specialised form of treatment, the patient has to be monitored very closely during the process to control the withdraw al effects. Often patients are so far down the road that it is decided that they cannot live without some form of drug to support their system so a mild sedative such as Tranqzine may be prescribed. The effects of too fast a withdrawal may be devastating to the patient so the whole process can take months.

Another area of treatment which was common in early years of addiction therapy was the psychological process of peeling off the layers of a patient's persona to find the source of the addiction and start the treatment from there. This resulted in many cases in the cause being discovered but the effect was not treated and the addict continued his or her abuse. Even if the cause is discovered and discussed it does not automatically mean that the addiction will go away. CDC do not recommend this treatment as it often causes more harm than good, it can be used once the patient is fully on the road to recovery, but CDC have to be totally sure that that is the road to take otherwise a relapse may occur. CDC encourage people to look at the contributing factors to their addiction such as life style and access to the addiction which will block their ability to recover rather than the causes.

Here it must be stressed that in a number of cases abusers of drugs or alcohol are not *'addicts'* as such but merely for some reason or other abuse the substances without losing total control over their bodies. It is taken as fact that once the patient has completed the initial screening process and has been diagnosed as an addict then the treatment starts from that point.

This category of addicts are those who have had their addiction thrust upon them either by the privileged position they occupy or a ready access to large sums of money. This is very common in divorced couples, bereavement and business failure, or the retired professional man who has been active until 65 and dies at 67 through cirrhosis of the liver, a common and relatively unknown area of addiction. A huge number of the latter example can be found in the Costa Del Sol and Costa Brava where lack of anything to do and the ready access to cheap alcohol or drugs creates whole communities of addicts. Whatever the cause of the addiction the habit takes on its own functional autonomy.

These patients can be treated earlier merely by the counsellor pointing out that they have developed a pattern of chemical abuse which could lead to addiction if it gets out of control.

A self-help guide for you to spot the habit in its early stages is; does your partner have a drink as soon as she or he comes home, are you entertaining a lot, is the off licence bill high, is your spouse coming home late, is he or she having the extra one before dinner. All these signs insignificant in themselves but can build into a problem.

Research has shown that children of alcoholic mothers are very likely to become heavy drinkers, especially if that mother has continued drinking throughout the pregnancy. The problem may also be inherited through the father or mother.

Once it has been established the type of abuse the addict is using, the severity of the addiction and his general health and mental state then treatment can begin. There is no cure for addiction CDC aims for abstinence to control the problem.

There is a great fear among addicts that as soon as they are admitted to any centre that they will immediately be labelled as mentally ill and remain incarcerated for the rest of their life. CDC see addiction as an illness in its own right and therefore the aim of the Centre is to reassure these people at a very early stage and give them hope for the future. Often an addict will prefer any other label than alcoholic or drug addict. CDC will look at whether there are contributory factors to the addiction such as sex, eating, sloth, idleness, workaholicism or gambling and integrate them as part of the cure process.

If these addictions occur without the presence of alcohol CDC recommend that they are dealt with separately by experts in their own fields. A list of these is available at the end of the book. Once the addict has been established and treatment is under way his or her family will attend weekly sessions & lectures with him or her to discuss the problem. Hopefully the family will already have had considerable counselling themselves. A great deal of addiction centres will only deal with the problem and not run any form of follow up therapy forth addict and his or her family.

Beware of any psychiatrist or therapist who recommends divorce as a way out of the addiction, the lawyer is the only professional who will not meet both parties and the cunning of the addict in these circumstances in hiding the addiction leads to lies and falsehoods being told about the other party. Beware of the lawyer who recommends any type of allegation be it sexual or violence to resolve the problem.

Once the addict has completed the treatment and realise that it is not possible for them ever to drink again he or she should take their new family life one step at a time. If both parties decide to split, then make the arrangements through a conciliator first before seeing a lawyer, Hilary Halpin deals with this aspect in great detail in Chapter 8.

But don't forget that time is a great healer and that you did love that person once and the alternative is the destruction of the family that you both have built up.

I can see that you are already confused as to how to spot your spouse being an addict, you may have spotted a similarity in yourself. To enable you to spot the problem we will invent a family called Peter and Sara who have just got married live in London and have no children.

Case Study – Peter and Sara

Peter is a Lloyd's insurance broker running his own company which is doing very well. He comes from an upper middle class family, his father was a stockbroker and mother from a wealthy property family. Unfortunately, his mother has recently spent a lot of time in hospital following addiction to sleeping pills. His father has retired and is just coping with the problem by having a house keeper and drinking rather more than he should.

Sara comes from an upper middle class family of bankers. She doesn't get on with Peter's family so they spend more time with her family. The women of her family, she has three sisters, are all very beautiful all married very well. Sadly her father had to retire early due to ill-health, a stress related illness, and her parents now live quietly in the country. Her mother comes up to London a lot and Sara has a very good relationship with her, she likes Peter and they often stay in the country. As both families enjoy parties the engagement was a great period for parties and dinners, a whirlwind time which caused Peter to ignore his job slightly but not with disastrous results. The wedding, for 250 people, was at Sara's country home with Bollinger champagne and the best food.

A dance afterwards for the younger generation ended at 4am when Peter and Sara went to their honeymoon in the West Indies. Peter was a very happy man, he had married a rich and very glamorous girl, his business was thriving and soon they would be moving into their new London house. Sara cooked directors' lunches and she would continue that as long as they had no children. The engagement had been great fun with only one or two incidents where Sara lost her temper but Peter put this down to pre-marital stress. Both his parents adored her, his brother, a wealthy banker and his wife had planned a joint holiday in the West Indies the next year.

The West Indies was marvellous, they drank, eat and swam all day. On their return to reality and married bliss they started planning the house move. Once moved in, Peter won a new contract and started coming back very late after long meetings with clients. It was after one of these meetings that he noticed that the plans for the new house were faltering and they were still living in a building site. He mentioned this to Sara and a fierce row ensued, she said that she couldn't work and do the house and he would have to let her give up her job and give her more time to do the house. Peter agreed and also gave her a bigger allowance. Eventually the house was finished and they had a grand house warming party for 120 guests.

At the end of the party when everyone had left Sara suddenly flew into a rage and said that she objected to him staying out all night working when she was slaving at home; she also accused him of drinking too much and that he should watch himself. Peter hadn't thought that he was drinking but agreed to lay off it for a while and join a Health Club. Sara was already a member of a smart tennis club and she had met a lot of women with husbands with a similar problem.

They were asked up to Scotland for a grouse shooting house party in August which they both decided would be a good break. The holiday was an active holiday with shooting beginning early in the morning with breakfast at eight. The evening dinners were full of good food and drink and usually finished in the early hours of the morning. The second day of the holiday Sara said that she wouldn't be coming with Peter to the hill and would stay in bed until lunch time as she was still tired from the house move. Peter had a good morning on the hill stopping at eleven o'clock for a well-earned gin & tonic, he got back to the shooting hut at lunch time to find a radiant Sara socialising and laughing arranging lunch with the other girls. She decided that she would go out shooting in the afternoons for the rest of the fortnight and spent the rest of the time shopping in Edinburgh and gossiping wither girlfriends.

They returned home after a great time to find that the inevitable had happened, Sara was pregnant. Peter was over the moon but he noticed a slight reticence in Sara's joy, he put it down to fear. He had told her that on no account must she drink during the pregnancy as his grandmother had with the result that his father was born with a weak liver and a penchant for the booze.

Sara agreed but became more and more aggressive over the following two weeks, Peter sent her to the doctor who said that everything was all right, merely a hormonal change. Sara demanded more and more money for baby clothes, prams and nurseries; Peter didn't mind as his business was doing very well and he wanted only the best for his first child. They booked into the Portland Hospital where all Sara's friends had their children. Peter was very excited by the prospect of becoming a father and decided to be present at the birth. Thomas arrived in the early morning after an easy birth, but Sara seemed very distant and took little notice, and he put it down to the early hour. Sara came out of hospital after three days and gradually became the confident mother.

Peter noticed a slight change in mood but was never there to tell the health visitor who always turned up when he was at work, the monthly nurse said that Sara might have a mild dose of Post Natal Depression. Once the monthly nurse had gone and the health visitor's visits became less frequent, Sara started complaining that her body had lost all it shape and she demanded a holiday and a course at the local health club. Peter agreed, and they went to Barbados leaving Thomas with a nanny. On their return the nanny was employed full time and Sara didn't go back to work. Peter noticed another distinct change, they were going out a lot and entertaining three nights a week and always planning week-end parties. Peter seemed to be doing most of the work with Thomas, as Sara wouldn't get up to do the early morning feed. His business began to suffer and he started drinking more than normal as Sara's moods became intolerable. He consulted his GP who said that he was overworking and drinking too much. He stopped but Sara continued the parties. Eventually after another late night Peter lost his temper and demanded that they stay in at least two nights a week with Thomas. Sara agreed for a while but then began to take cooking jobs again doing a lot of cocktail parties.

With the added strain of the relationship Peter's company then failed and had to be bought out with Peter becoming an employee again. Large cutbacks had to be made, Sara's clothes allowance and Club memberships were ditched and the nanny only came twice a week thus Sara had to stay in.

Her moods became intolerable and they started argu-ing with both of them throwing things at each other. The GP put it down to the strain of Peter's business going wrong and did nothing. But the GP did decide to see Sara and prescribed a course of sleeping pills to combat the lack of sleep which in her opinion caused Sara's mood swings. Sara began the course and slept well for a number of weeks but after one course decided that to be on the safe side she needed a further course, the GP agreed and she was on the pills for a year.

Subsequently Sara became disinterested in sex and Peter became more intolerant and took to staying out late with his male friends or working. The moods returned and Peter went down to ask his mother's advice who said that it happened in many families especially theirs, Sara was very like her mother, it would soon pass, in the meantime they would help out with a full time nanny. Stability returned for a while until Peter came back early from work one day to find Sara fast asleep in the chair with an empty bottle of wine by the chair. Thomas was crying having been dropped by Sara and the nanny said that Sara had thrown a tantrum and threatened to sack the nanny for being slack. It became clear that the nanny had known for some time that Sara had been drinking.

Peter was furious and rang his lawyer to set up a deed of separation as he had had enough. He was furious with himself that he had not noticed the danger signs earlier, his work had been ruined and now his marriage was on the rocks. He stormed out of the house and went down to the pub. Luckily for Peter he met a friend who had had a similar experience and put Peter in touch with a clinic. He told him to cancel his meeting with the lawyer and to concentrate on getting Sara well. Sara was admitted to the clinic and after several months' treatment she was on the road to recovery; she stopped drinking, the mood swings have gone, she had more energy, her thought patterns were clearer and she adores Thomas and Peter. Peter attended a number of family therapy sessions with Sara and also had counselling for his workaholicism.

Sara is now fully recovered attending regular AA meetings, Peter is a member of Al-Anon and doing his own counselling whilst for Thomas life goes on unbeknown to him that his whole life nearly changed for the worst but for the intervention of a friend and an understanding therapist.

The complexity of Sara's case, the initial denial, the cover-up by the cooking jobs, the loss of self-esteem after the birth and the cross addiction to the sleeping pills required a long and tough course.

This story is a fabricated case study which has compressed all the experiences I have been told into one story. From the study above, you will be able to spot that the illness began at a very early stage in Sara & Peter's relationship, it is certain that it was there before they married, the hereditary habits of both their families shielded the problem as both Peter and Sara had been brought up in a family unit where alcohol and argument was the norm.

Peter's workaholic type was very suited to Sara's alcoholism and they had become co-dependent until Sara's addiction got out of control.

Case Study – John

John was happily married to his wife Anne, both families came from wealthy backgrounds and money was no problem. Half way into their marriage John realised that Anne was taking drugs. His family had a history of alcohol abuse and he was terrified of the pattern repeating itself. He begged Anne to stop and she got worse and worse. One day she swore to him that she would stop the habits she was now taking hard drugs. Her health deteriorated and she was on death's door. Suddenly one day she disappeared without warning to a clinic and came back eight weeks later radiant and recovered.

She was the belle of the ball and all going out to parties again. John meanwhile could not handle the recovery and slipped into a pattern of drinking which eventually led to divorce. He continued the abuse for two years after the divorce himself ending up in a treatment centre. Both are now happily remarried and neither abusing any form of drug or alcohol.

Chapter 6

Stress Recognition, Exercising the Option

Alicia Trevor B.A. Hons, Fitness Consultant

Stress is a killer, it lurks hidden for many years manifesting itself in later years in the form of heart disease, strokes or cancer. Stressful situations created at work can often be solved when fellow colleagues notice a change in the person's work patterns. There is now a well-established league table of stressful jobs with doctors, journalists and lawyers numbering among the top places. The majority of large corporations and businesses have recognised stress in the workplace and have initiated a number of programmes to help sufferers not so much as a result of sympathy towards the sufferer but more following the huge financial costs caused by stress amongst the workforce.

In a vast number of cases stress is followed by alcohol addiction as the majority of stress sufferers will use alcohol as a means of giving a *'quick fix'* solution to the problem. Alcohol is a depressant and will therefore often increase stress levels. Thus, the sufferer will often be treated for alcoholism by a *'drying out'* process rather than primarily having tackled the cause of the stress.

Stress factors to-day in the domestic arena are far higher than years ago due to the increased risk of unemployment, loss of home, increased divorce rate and the general high cost of living. Childbirth is the most stressful time for both parents and with the growing trend of women working the result has been that some of these women will go back to work too early to the detriment of their family and health. This scenario is very common in the arena of the professional woman having children later on in life who believes that her ability to cope with stresses in the workplace will give her the automatic ability to cope with a small child. Unfortunately, small children are unpredictable and will wake up at all hours and become ill or hurt themselves at short notice.

If this mother then goes back to work too early she will often shield the stress by drinking on the way home, this has been proved by domestic violence surveys which show that violence commonly occurs after 7 PM, that is after the children have been put to bed and the mother's stress levels and fatigue are at their highest. The husband has returned home from work and he too is tired and has a drink and wants his food. It is the recognition of this stress factor in both parties at a very early stage which will prevent the problem escalating to dependence on alcohol or drugs or domestic violence. If you see your partner suffering from stress, plan an initial programme of early nights for both of you, less parties and alcohol and less late nights at the office for the husband.

If the problem is unresolvable by these means and your partner does not recognise that she is suffering from stress, then discuss the problem with the GP and initiate a programme for yourself. Continuing stress will show through in reduced mental performance at work and home, it is far easier to deal with a stressful partner if the other partner is in control.

Many wives will consider your request for them to visit the doctor as a hint that they are suffering from some kind of mental illness, so suggest that you both join a local health club where you can exercise and meet new people. Research over recent years has collated evidence that suggests exercise has many beneficial properties including those of reducing stress, anxiety and depression. It is therefore no longer unusual to find a physician who will prescribe exercise rather than drugs to combat the stresses of modern life. In a survey of 1750 physicians, 80% reported doing exactly that for the relief of depression. [Ryan 1983]

Regular visits to your gym may enable you and your partner to experience for yourselves an increased ability to cope without the need to consult a doctor. It must be said that exercise may not be the most beneficial medium for you - many people may find relaxation more efficacious or a combination of the two (See Chapter 8).

It has often been hypothesised that social interaction with new people can help elevate negative mood states, as loneliness is often a contributing factor or symptom of stress. Joining a Health Club will naturally provide opportunities to meet new people and make new friends therefore helping to alleviate negative moods. Your partner may then see for herself that the exercise is creating a better ability to cope with the stresses of life.

So what constitutes a programme of stress management? Do you run five miles a day and come off fatty foods and drink water all day, NO! Discuss your problems with the Fitness Consultant at the Health Club and she or he will give you a programme suited to your individual needs.

Before undertaking your exercise programme, the fitness consultant should ensure that there are no physical reasons why you should not exercise. A brief medical history may be required along with a blood pressure check to determine a critical level of health. All good health clubs should offer this service but if not please consult your doctor first.

As elevated blood pressure is a common symptom of stress it is not unlikely that you will be referred back to your doctor and asked to provide a doctor's certificate to show that it is safe for you to exercise. If you are found to be suffering from high blood pressure DO NOT WORRY. In some instances such as physical incapacitation the Fitness Consultant may consider it inappropriate for you to use the gym for stress reduction and will recommend relaxation therapy (see Chapter 7) Research indicates that both relaxation therapy and physical exercise are both highly effective for the reduction of stress dependant on the individual concerned.

But how is stress recognised and how is it combated in the early stages:

Psychological symptoms

- Feeling unable to cope and make decisions

- Irritability

- Lethargy/Disinterest in life

- Constant/Recurrent fear of disease - Low self-esteem

- Inability to make decisions

- Feelings of ugliness

- Suppression of Rage/Anger, due to inability to show true feelings

- Anxiety

- Depression

- Inability to make decisions

- Excessive dependence on alcohol and/or tobacco and/or drugs

Physiological Symptoms

- Lack of appetite but craving for food under pressure

- Tiredness but insomnia

- Indigestion/Heartburn/Nausea

- Reduced resistance to disease

- Constipation/Diarrhoea

- Tendency to sweat without reason

- High Blood Pressure

- Headaches

- Nail biting/Fidgeting

- Crying/Desire to cry

- Impotence/Frigidity

- Fainting spells

- Breathlessness without exertion

- Cramps/Muscle spasm

Suggestions to combat stress:

Make a list of all stressors in your life and learn to recognise them. Sit down and work out ways to deal with these stressors e.g.

- Limit your working week to 5 days, 6 at most. No more than 10 hours/day

- Keep 1 day completely free of routine work

- Cultivate a hobby, relax, exercise

- Don't over commit

- Don't shoulder other people's responsibilities

- Seek advice on problems

- Prioritise tasks and focus on one at a time

- Be honest; say how you feel and speak your mind (in moderation!)

Insomnia

Insomnia deserves special treatment as a great number of stress sufferers have to contend with sleepless nights.

DON'T attempt to sleep unless you are unwound and relaxed - this will only cause worry therefore preventing any chance of your doing so.

It is imperative to reduce muscular tension before attempting to sleep either by practising tension relief techniques or simply by taking *'time-out'* and indulging in a warm bath or sitting down with a hot drink.

Relaxation is a skill we must learn, so perhaps take time out to attend a class. Use this time to vacate the mind and shut out work and other stressors.

AVOID: CAFFEINE (tea, coffee, coke etc.)
NICOTINE
ALCOHOL
EATING LATE

Before resorting to drugs as many do, consider other factors which may be preventing a sound sleep e.g. the environment

- Bed too hard/soft

- Room too hot/cold

- Heavy covers

- Partner snoring or hogging the bed; perhaps try separate rooms

Drugs do not induce a normal sleep pattern and so the sufferer may still feel tired and hung-over the next morning.

It may help to make a list of everyday irritations that create problems which can be resolved for instance if you are always late or constantly rushing around in the mornings, make sure you organise your clothes, briefcase, sports kit etc. before going to bed. **THIS MAY SOUND SIMPLE BUT IT WORKS!**

Accompanying stress, if the problem is not spotted early, there will be a propensity for the stress sufferer to develop depression of which there are two types, state and trait.

STATE - Due to cause and effect, results from external factors such as divorce or loss of job reflects such short term feelings.

TRAIT - A predisposition may result from genetic factors or a chemical imbalance.

Recent research suggests that physical exercise stimulates the production and release of endorphins - endogenous opioids - which act as natural painkillers and induce feelings of wellbeing. Studies have shown these natural opioids to be two hundred times more powerful than comparable doses of morphine.

Beta-endorphins, a subdivision of the central nervous system opioids group, are activated by prolonged exercise and are released from the pituitary gland simultaneously with ACTH (ADRENOCORTROPHIC hormone). On examination, many researchers have found an increase in peripheral blood beta-endorphin concentration within plasma samples following exercise, concurrent with elevated mood states. Similar results have been found in experiments with rats where in exercising the beta-endorphin levels were still elevated 48 hours post cessation of the exercise but had descended to normal after 98 hours.

Elevations in body temperature have been found to induce therapeutic benefits such as decreased depression and anxiety but this theory has been found to be flawed as exceeding an optimum level of heat in itself causes stress. Again, sufferers should take care when trying this type of treatment in saunas and steam rooms as over use especially with people with heart or alcohol problems can result in severe illness or death in extreme cases. The great *'Dell Boy'* theory of the hot curry and a sauna after a skin full of alcohol should be avoided at all costs as the increased temperature of the sauna will put undue pressure on your heart which is already working overtime to clean the body of the excess alcohol. It must be stressed that the liver can only process 7gms of alcohol an hour thus no form of increased exercise or heat will increase the disposal of the alcohol.

It has been suggested that the positive mood shifts associated with regular exercise cannot be explained merely by one theory alone. The concept of several physiological and psychological mechanisms at work simultaneously is now widely advocated. Research has indicated that for some - accompanying the positive physiological reactions to exercise - merely taking *'time out'* from a daily routine has a positive effect. Actually, going to a gym and spending time away from a normal routine will divert the mind away from that which is causing the initial problem. Many people may have a very negative attitude towards exercise for whatever reason. However, it has been found that those who perceive exercise to be stressful or unenjoyable before participation in a regular regime may experience a more favourable attitude change towards it. This may be due to actual or anticipated benefit derived from exercise such as increased well-being and self-esteem.

Self-esteem, self-efficacy and self-mastery are all concepts which are inextricably linked. Goal achievement such as exercise participation will inspire the above *'self'* variables and in turn act as an incentive for the individual to tackle other areas in their life in need of attention e.g. that which is causing the stress or depression. After several weeks the regular exerciser should experience change which reinforces and justifies their participation. As well as enhanced mental well-being physiological changes such as weight control, muscle tone etc. may occur. These changes often inspire confidence and allow the individual greater control in other aspects of their lives. It should be noted that the key word here is *'regular.'*

Research has demonstrated that individuals with greater exercise frequency were more efficacious and emotionally stable. For those individuals who do not have the confidence to start exercising immediately at a gym it may be an idea to exercise at home initially. The real efficacy of exercise has never been fully explained and researchers suggest that other factors have to be taken into account before a picture can be established.

For example:

1. Type of exercise e.g. aerobic or anaerobic.

2. Duration e.g. 8 and 30 minutes or between 30 and 60 minutes.

3. Frequency - 3 to 5 times per week recommended.

4. Intensity - Moderate - 60%of heart rate max or high intensity 70-85% of heart rate max.

5. Adherence - Continuing participation increase benefits derived from exercise with time. [Dishmar 1982]

6. Personality - Studies have shown that those who held a more positive attitude towards exercise for the purpose of health and fitness, had a decreased state of anxiety and depression post exercise significantly more than those with more neutral attitudes.

Evidence suggests that aerobic exercise is more efficacious than anaerobic exercise in reducing negative mood states. Results show that exercise acts as a redactor of anxiety, but only with the use of aerobic forms, not anaerobic.

The benefits derived from exercise and how quickly they will be felt will depend very much on the individual and the above factors. As was stated earlier, before undertaking any form of exercise you must be 100% sure that you are physically up to it. Please check your suitability with your doctor first and take his professional advice.

Obviously, a programme needs to be tailored to each individual so do not attempt to devise your own fitness programme but ask professional advice. All good gyms should offer you a personalised programme free of charge. Particularly for those who have little exercise experience, it may be beneficial to engage a Personal Trainer in the early days. It is important to check that your Personal Trainer is qualified and insured should anything untoward occur.

Saving the Situation

Given proper instruction there should be little danger, provided that you have a clean bill of health and that any special medical advice has been followed.

A good Personal Trainer will research your requirements and ensure that you are getting the correct amount of exercise every step of the way. They are there throughout your session to look after you on a one-to-one basis with no interruptions. If you find it too expensive to have your trainer for every session, at least consider a trainer for the first few sessions to ensure that you are on the right road.

The National Registry of Personal Trainers will provide a list of qualified instructors in your area or contact Alicia Trevor for further information.

Regular use of the above routines will leave you in a much better frame of mind to face the problems at home. Should the problems at home become insuperable and break -up of the family occurs it is vital that you continue the exercise programme as the stress resulting from family break up and divorce often forces the victim to start down the same slippery slope as the stressed or depressed person.

At the same time that you are utilising the stress programmes, look at your diet. There are several components in many peoples' diets which tend to exacerbate the many symptoms of stress. It is therefore recommended that these substances are limited in any quantities, if not cut out altogether.

CAFFEINE
Increases blood pressure
Increases blood sugar levels
Contracts the muscles leading to tenseness

SODIUM (salt)
Increases blood pressure

NICOTINE
Increases heart rate
Constricts blood vessels thus increased blood pressure

TYPICAL LIFE EVALUATION SHEET

WHAT DO YOU WANT TO ACHIEVE IN YOUR LIFE

_____

_____

_____

WHY ARE WE HERE AND FOR WHAT PURPOSE?

_____

_____

_____

RE-APPRAISE YOUR AMBITIONS AND PRIORITISE YOUR GOALS

ENJOY THE JOURNEY AS MUCH AS THE DESTINATION

IT IS IMPORTANT TO TAKE TIME TO ENJOY THE THINGS ALONG THE WAY TO OUR ULTIMATE GOALS. IF WEARE NOT HERETO ENJOY OURSELVES THEN WHY BOTHER?

ONLY SET OUT TO ACCOMPLISH WHAT YOU WANT/ NEED TO ACHIEVE

REMEMBER: QUALITY NOT QUANTITY

Chapter 7

Relaxation for Living
How to Cope with the Stresses of a
Difficult Relationship

Susan Balfour, Relaxation for Living

'Stress is anything that makes a demand on the human being to
adapt or adjust or change in some way.'
Dr Hans Selye, *The Stress of Life*

All change is stressful, but because we are adaptive human
beings we can adjust to a certain number of changes without
experiencing any adverse effect. There is however a limit; if
we go beyond that limit our adaptive capacity is thrown into
overload and we feel we can no longer cope.

Too Much Change is Stressful

In a situation of divorce or relationship breakdown many
changes and adjustments are forced upon the individuals
involved be they the wife, husband or children. For the man
there is often a change of residence; a change of status from
being one of a couple to being a single person again; there
is a change in financial status as he attempts to maintain
two households; and, perhaps more importantly, there is a
change in the way he relates to his partner and she to him -
both, as well as the children, have lost the support, love and

friendship that was such a source of comfort before things started to go wrong.

This, in turn often causes a change in the way the individual relates to himself. Doubts about one's value and worth begin to take hold, he frequently feels unlovable to anybody and a negative change in self-image and self-esteem ensues.

There is often change in one's social life - friends may take sides, and even if they take your side they not may feel comfortable with inviting you as a single person. You have become a threat to the status quo and it is easier to ignore you than to deal with the change demanded in relating to you as a separate individual. Changing one's perceptions is stressful and most people would rather not have any more stress than is absolutely necessary. So invitations dwindle and a feeling of being a social outcast sets in.

Changes also occur, of course, in the number and type of chores you have to cope with. You may suddenly have to take on the activities which were the domain of your partner such as shopping, cooking, washing clothes, visiting the laundrette, housework and looking after the children. This may be quite a shock if you have taken it for granted that these time-consuming chores will be handled by someone else. So you will probably need to reorganise your weekly timetable to take these new demands into account.

One of the first steps in managing the stress of separation or breakups is to make a conscious list of how many things have changed - how many things are you going to have to readjust to, along the lines of the list given above.

With this list in mind, try to minimise any other changes in your life. Do not make any unnecessary changes on top of the ones that are beyond your control. Remember you can cope with a certain number of changes but there is a limit beyond which your adaptive capacity will be stretched to breaking point and this is when one small extra demand can throw you into crisis and feeling that you cannot cope at all. According to Dr Hans Selye, every individual is born with a certain amount of *"adaption energy"*. It is something like a bag of coins; once spent, it cannot be replaced. So, make sure you do not spend all your adaption energy, keep some in reserve. One of the signals that you have reached your limit is when most things feel like a strain to do. So as soon as you feel strained by the demands of your life, you must stop and take time off to rest and pamper yourself.

This is very important - you must constantly replenish your reserves, one of the most fundamental ways of doing this is by rest, sleep and relaxation. These are not luxuries, they are absolute essentials if you are going to come through extreme stress without permanent damage.

Has Your Efficiency Deteriorated?

Another way to monitor whether you have reached your limit is to look at your efficiency level. Has your efficiency deteriorated? If you are close to this critical line, your efficiency rapidly falls, event below zero. This means that with too much stress you can actually become counterproductive - worse than useless! Up to a certain point in creased effort produces increased efficiency, but beyond that critical line even the addition of a minor task could be enough to push you past your peak and on to a downward slope. When you are in that state, even things you normally do well will be beyond your grasp. When you notice your efficiency has deteriorated you must take steps to relax more, take more time off just to *"potter"*, and to take time off for pleasant, recreational pursuits.

You Need Pleasure and Recreation

Look at those two words *'pleasant'* and *'recreational.'* Pleasant pursuits give you pleasure. Pleasure is a human need and one that is in short supply in the acrimonious and painful situation of divorce or relationship breakdown. You must take time to balance the scales a little and seek out people who care for you and give you a positive response and positive feedback about yourself and make time for activities that you enjoy.

The other word *'recreational'* means to re-create yourself; replenish yourself. Give time to activities and people that *'nourish'* you – that make you feel renewed. An inexpensive way of replenishing yourself may be a walk in the park or by the river - it doesn't have to cost money - you could also indulge yourself by taking time to read the newspapers for longer than you normally would, or to read a book you've always wanted to read but thought you never had time for.

This kind of distraction is restful to the mind as it takes it away from going round and round the problems you are facing and the distress you feel. Give yourself permission to take time off from the problem. Try to seek out people with whom you can have fun, go to the gym (see Chapter 6) or rent a funny video to give your mind a break. It will be more creative when you turn back to dealing with the problem.

Are You Tense? Tension is Tiring

When we are under extreme stress we usually become tense. We tense up muscles in an extra effort to cope, but this extra effort merely wears us out as tension is tiring and does not solve anything. A tense muscle is using energy and when we have unnecessary tension in our bodies we are wasting valuable energy - energy that could be used more positively. It is so easy, in a crisis situation to strive too hard and when one has been at the tense, striving end of the spectrum, we need to learn to stop for periods of time and do absolutely nothing.

We need to put ourselves at the other end of the spectrum - the nondoing, passive pole. We may need to be inactive for considerable periods of time in order to restore the balance and restore the body's energy supplies. So, do not be too harsh with yourself if you find that you do not feel like doing as much as you used to - this is not a permanent state - it is just that you are worn out and exhausted by too many changes, too much to adapt to and most probably by striving too hard to sort things out.

I cannot emphasise enough the importance of taking a break, resting and practising relaxation techniques. When we are deeply relaxed, with no tension in the muscles, the body can re-energise and revitalise itself more completely, and the immune system also works more effectively when we are in a state of deep relaxation.

The more exhausted you are, the less resources you have to cope. A chronically fatigued person will see life's demands as threats rather than as interesting challenges to his creativity.

Practicing a relaxation routine in times of stress is essential to helping you to get through the day. At other times it is a very useful preventative measure against burn-out and negative thinking. At the end of this chapter a routine will be demonstrated for switching off the hard working muscles and putting yourself in a state of deep relaxation. You should practice this routine every day for half an hour. As well as practicing this relaxation routine, you should watch yourself very carefully for when you are using too much tension - remember this wears you out and wastes your energy.

How Much Effort Are You Putting In?

Try to be aware of how much effort (or tension) you are putting into all the tasks you perform each day. How tightly do you hold the steering wheel when you are driving? Do you have the right amount of tension in your grip - or is it too much? Are you gripping so tightly that your knuckles are white? How tightly do hold the telephone? Again, do you grip it with all your might as if it were a ten ton weight? How tightly do you need to hold a pen in order to control it across the page? Does tightening your grip help you to write faster - no.it does not! It merely tires you more quickly than necessary. Only use the amount of tension that is needed for the task in hand - using ten times that amount will not speed you up or increase your intelligence. It will slow you down eventually and exhaust you, rendering you less able to think intelligently and creatively.

Another reason for monitoring your tension level is because extreme tension in the muscles will send signals of alarm to your brain and will cause the fight or flight response to be switched on internally (see Chapter 3). When we are in a state of stress all kinds of changes take place in our bodies in order to help us to cope better with the stressful situation. These changes, however, are only intended to be activated for a short burst of activity to get us *away* from the stress. They are not supposed to be maintained over long periods of time, as they put a great strain on the body.

The Stress Response

The stress response is known as the *'fight or flight'* response because it is designed to help us fight or flee our way out of difficulty; but most modern problems are not solved in this way. The body, however, has only one way of responding to a perceived problem or threat and upon receiving messages from the brain that something is wrong it gears itself up for action. Our stress responses are programmed for when we lived in a more primitive state and most stresses were life or death threats. Now that we have become *'civilised'* the enemy has changed, and we need to switch off the internal stress responses that once may have saved our lives, but which now do not usually help with our modern problems and can in fact shorten our lives.

It is important to understand what changes are taking place in your body when you are under stress. When you realise how potentially harmful these stress responses can be if they are left switched on for long periods - or constantly - it will give you the motivation to practice the deep relaxation and other stress reduction techniques that you are being given you in this chapter.

You can be in control, you do not need to be the victim of uncontrolled *'fight or flight'* responses that will raise your blood pressure, alter much of your body chemistry and burn you out - or worse!

Knowledge of how your body works in the modern context is critical to your ability to conquer and even thrive on stress. Unthinking reflexes must now give way to a thoughtful response and an intelligently planned strategy.

Deep Relaxation Routine

The Relaxation Response

Lie down on a firm sofa, bed or the floor. Have a small cushion under your head and place a large cushion or pillow under your thighs to take the strain off your abdomen and ease the small of your back. Make sure that you are warm as you cannot relax completely if you are cold. It is a good idea to cover yourself with a rug or blanket, as your body temperature drops when you relax deeply, because your heart rate slows down a little and your blood pressure drops. This is why regular practice of deep relaxation is especially good for anyone with high blood pressure problems.

Then:

1. Become aware of your shoulders and pull them down towards your hips (the opposite of shrugging), hold them stretched down for a few seconds and then let them go.

2. Become aware of your arms. Move your arms a little away from the sides of your body, so that your elbows are bent outwards. Let your hands rest on your tummy, or by your sides. Now push your arms down into the support (the sofa, bed or floor), hold for a moment and then stop pushing. Feel your arms getting heavier. Let go more and more through the muscles in your arms.

Feel them being completely held by the support. Let go a little more.

3. Now be aware of your hands. With your hands still supported, either beside you, or on your tummy, stretch out your fingers and thumbs. Hold the stretch for a few seconds and then let your fingers flop. Let them be limp, not holding on to anything, and feel your hands completely still and relaxed.

4. Now be aware of your legs. Let your legs fall slightly apart, so that your knees roll outwards. Now press your legs down into the support - hold for a few seconds, then let go. Feel your legs sinking down a little more. Feel your legs becoming heavier and relaxed.

5. Now be aware of your tummy muscles. As you breathe out let your tummy muscles go. Let your tummy muscles feel loose and limp and easy - no holding on.

6. Now be aware of your diaphragm - just above your waist. Feel as if this part of you is expanding slightly. Just let go all around the middle.

7. Now be aware of your back being supported. Press down a little more heavily into the support, hold for a few seconds, and then let go. Feel your whole body being held a little more completely than before. Now let go more deeply.

8. Now be aware of your mouth and jaw. Make sure your top and bottom teeth are slightly apart, not clenched together. Let your tongue drop down to the bottom of

your mouth, behind your bottom teeth. Do not have your tongue clamped to the roof of your mouth - this is the tense position. Now make sure that you are not clenching your lips. Let your lips be just lightly touching. Become aware of how it feels to have a relaxed mouth and jaw.

9. Now be aware of your eyes. Let your eyelids be lightly closed. Let your eye muscles relax - there is nothing to stare at or focus on - let your eye muscles relax.

10. Now be aware of your forehead. Feel as if gentle fingers are smoothing your forehead outwards from the centre towards the temples. Feel as if your forehead is widening. Feel as if all the worry lines are being smoothed away.

11. Now feel as if your forehead is being gently smoothed upwards from your eyebrows to your hairline. Feel as if your forehead is getting higher. Feel as if you have a high, wide brow that feels calm and smooth.

12. Now imagine gentle hands are massaging over your scalp. Feel as if your head area is expanding a little. Let go through all the muscles in your scalp - relax your scalp and head.

13. Now just enjoy the feeling of being relaxed. Enjoy the feeling of ease. Enjoy the feeling of calm that comes with letting go.

14. Stay with this relaxed feeling and picture a beautiful peaceful place somewhere you would like to be. Rest in this beautiful place for a few moments, in order to

rest and refresh your mind. Enjoy being there. Enjoy taking a little time off from the outside world and be aware that this is a very healthy thing to do. You are not wasting time - you are using time very creatively to restore your energy and vitality. Remember that all the repair mechanisms of the body are enhanced, and the immune system boosted, when we are in a state of deep relaxation.

You might like to record this relaxation routine onto an audio cassette or buy one of the number available direct from Relaxation for Living.

What happens to the body in the stress response

The Physical responses to stress

1. **The Racing heartbeat**

   The heart beats more rapidly than usual to pump more blood to the large muscles and the lungs in order that you have more fuel and oxygen to fight or flee from a perceived danger. The rapid heartbeat is often switched on for long periods of time when one is stressed, this can lead to high blood pressure which if unchecked could lead to strokes or other problems such as a heart attack. The extra stress factor could be the one that pushes you over the edge. If you have family history of heart problems or poor lifestyle habits have regular check-ups from your doctor.

2. **The blood thickens and hormonal and chemical changes occur**

There is increased production of red and white blood cells and clotting factors into the bloodstream, in order to provide more capacity to carry oxygen, to fight infections and to stop bleeding from a wound. Extra adrenalin is pumped into the system to keep the *'fight or flight'* response going (see Chapter 3) not useful if you are trying to sleep before an important Court case. It makes you feel *'high'* and super charged', but it is an artificial 'charge' and eventually burns you out. Extra cortisone is released from the adrenal gland as a protection, but again, if chronically elevated over long periods cortisone destroys the body's resistance to the stresses of illness. The lymph glands shrivel up and the immune response is weakened. The ability to fight off any form of illness is impaired. There is also an increased output of endorphins (see Chapter 6) which although a pain killer for physical wounds does not cure the emotional ones. Relentless stress can deplete the levels of endorphin, which may explain why emotional stress can cause us to avoid physical stress.

3. Reduction in sex hormones

The body's logic is that in a situation of extreme danger it is not appropriate to wish to procreate the human race or indulge in sexual pleasure thus there is a predictable decrease in sexual libido accompanying stress. If this is not understood it leads to obvious anxieties and failures when intercourse is attempted - as well as anxiety about the decrease in sexual desire. Regular relaxation or holidays will usually cure this problem.

4. Shutdown of the digestive system

The digestive system is shut down during periods of danger as the last thing you are likely to want to do is to sit down to eat. The blood is diverted away from the stomach to the muscles, and the *'engine room'* of the heart and lungs. The message to be taken from this is that it is highly undesirable to eat when you are stressed or churned up as you will not be able to digest your food properly. This is the reason people develop nervous indigestion and eventually stomach ulcers. Other symptoms can be stomach bloating, nausea, cramps, discomfort and even diarrhoea. Also the mouth goes dry, as the saliva has dried up, which is why public speakers are usually given a glass of water to hand, in anticipation of this particular response to *'nerves'*.

5. Release of extra blood sugar

Today's threats are mostly emotional and psychological and therefore the sugar released to be used for *'sprinting away from danger'* is not used up but simply makes excessive demands on the pancreas for extra insulin. Some doctors maintain that diabetes can be aggravated or started in this way. It can be understood why the stress response of eating an excess of foods high in sugar is damaging when the bloodstream already has high levels of sugar as part of its natural response to stress.

6. Breathing becomes rapid and shallow

This is in order to provide extra supplies of oxygen

to feed the increased blood supply coming into the lungs. This is useful when we exert ourselves, but not when we sit all tensed up in a state of anxiety or anger or hurt, we can then begin to hyperventilate, which is over breathing for the activity we are engaged in. Too much oxygen and too little carbon dioxide can cause strange sensations such as tingling in the finger tips or toes and can also cause feelings of breathlessness or feeling light headed. If these sensations are experienced you need to make an effort to breathe out for longer - like a sigh - then breathe in low down, into your diaphragm (just above your waist) and then breathe out again slowly and breathe in again slowly and low into your diaphragm. Practice this breathing pattern for a few minutes until you feel calmer. If you still feel strange and panicky it can help to breathe into a paper bag, so that you inhale your own carbon dioxide. If it continues make sure you carry a paper bag in your pocket.

7. The skin tingles, pales and sweats

The bristling of hairs when we are frightened heightens the sense of touch, acting much like a cat's whiskers, providing a sort of *'radar'* to detect our closest environment. The skin goes pale, because of diverting away from it the blood needed elsewhere. The skin also sweats, this is the body's cooling system and essential if running away but embarrassing in other circumstances. This combination of clammy hands, pasty face and stained armpits simply leads to increased feelings of stress and inadequacy!

8. Heightening our senses

In times of stress all our five senses become more acute. This brings the body into peak functioning for dealing with an emergency, but the long term effect is a high error rate. It seems that the senses burn out after unrelenting stress and become less efficient. The person be comes less observant of details around him or her, pays less attention to tastes or smells, tunes out whole conversations, and becomes less responsive to touch. Become aware when this error rate is high as this could save your life in such situations as driving, using tools and garden machines. Even pleasant or exciting emotions such as driving back from hospital with a new baby can be dangerous.

Conclusion check list

1. Be aware of how many changes you are having to cope with.

2. Do not make any unnecessary changes.

3. Take time off from the problem and seek out people who care for you and who give you positive feedback about yourself.

4. Remember that just because one person in your life has stopped loving you that does not mean you are unlovable, or that no one else will love or appreciate you.

5. Pamper yourself. You must now care for yourself and pampering yourself a little (or a lot) is a way of loving yourself and valuing yourself.

6. Practice deep relaxation for at least half an hour every day to restore your energy and your coping capacity.

7. Eat well to support yourself. Do not turn to negative coping strategies that will eventually undermine you, like alcohol or other artificial stimulants, junk snacks or too much sugar.

8. Get sufficient sleep and try to use relaxation techniques or a warm bath to put you in the mood for sleep, rather than relying on sleeping tablets.

9. Take time off from your problem (don't worry, it won't run away!) Try to get out into the fresh air and walk away and try to take some kind of gentle exercise to ease out the tension in the muscles, to burn off anger and to distract you. Swimming is one of the best forms of exercise.

10. Forgive yourself if your efficiency has deteriorated. This is just a passing phase until you readjust to the new circumstances of your life.

11. Do not neglect leisure and recreational time. Take time off to enjoy yourself and remember laughter is one of the best healers.

12. Do not try to sort everything out at once. Take one thing at a time and keep a perspective. You have plenty of time- and remember, time is another of life's great healers and that the current problem in your life will end one day.

Lastly forgive yourself.

Chapter 8

How the Police can Help Domestic Problems

Domestic violence occurs in all classes, creeds, and religions; the abuser can be male or female. Where actual violence occurs, that is physical harm, it is commonly recognised that the majority of victims are women.

Women have also been known to use baseball bats, bottles & chairs but by their very nature and build they tend to use more subtle means of domestic violence than brute force. Domestic violence also occurs between gay and lesbian couples.

The causes and effects of domestic violence are dealt with in greater detail in Chapter 2.

When actual violence occurs it is often the culmination of a situation where other forms of abuse have failed; either the victims striking back or the abuser is using brute force having failed to control his or her partner by other means. Studies have shown that in cases where men have suffered mental, economic or emotional abuse they will often use strength as the means of last resort. If violence occurs in the home visit your GP and explain the problem. If the abuser is female the man will receive very little sympathy from the GP, but it is an essential move as when the problem escalates and the Police are called they will use the GP as a reference.

- An estimated 1.9 million adults aged 16 to 59 years experienced domestic abuse in the last year, according to the year ending March 2017 Crime Survey for England and Wales (1.2 million women, 713,000 men).

- The police recorded 1.1 million domestic abuse-related incidents and crimes in the year ending March 2017 and of these, 46% were recorded as domestic abuse-related crimes; domestic abuse-related crimes recorded by the police accounted for 32% of violent crimes.

- There were 46 arrests per 100 domestic abuse-related crimes recorded by 39 police forces in the year ending June 2017.

- The majority of victims of domestic homicides recorded between April 2013 and March 2016 were females (70%).

- A decision to charge was made for 72% of domestic abuse-related cases referred to the Crown Prosecution Service (CPS) by the police, and of those that proceeded to court, convictions were secured for 76% of domestic abuse-related prosecutions.

- There were 305 refuge services operating in England and Wales in 2017.

- A total of 83,136 high-risk cases were discussed at

multi-agency risk assessment conferences in the year ending March 2017, equating to 36 cases per 10,000 adult females.

Summary

The different datasets included in this report do not relate to the same cases given the different timescales and reference periods used to collect the data. They also do not count the same things; for example, some record the number of victims or defendants, whilst others record the number of incidents or offences that occurred. Therefore, each of the numbers cannot be directly compared. However, it is apparent from the different sources that many victims do not see justice, with the majority of cases not coming to the attention of the police, and many of those that do come to their attention do not result in a conviction for the perpetrator of the abuse. This is illustrated in Figure 1 (not presented to scale).

Domestic abuse is often a hidden crime that is not reported to the police, which is why the estimated number of victims is much higher than the number of incidents and crimes recorded by the police. Of the cases which do come to the attention of the police, many, although still recorded as incidents and dealt with as required, will fall short of notifiable offences and are therefore not recorded as crimes.

Approximately half of domestic abuse-related crimes that are recorded by the police do not result in an arrest and a large proportion have evidential difficulties in proceeding with prosecution. Evidential difficulties often relate to the victim not supporting the prosecution. This reflects the challenges involved in investigating domestic abuse-related offences and demonstrates the importance of a robust evidence-led case being built for the victim.

Domestic abuse accounts for a significant proportion of the work carried out by both the police and the Crown Prosecution Service (11% of crimes recorded by the police and 16% of prosecutions), but there is variation across police force areas in the response to cases. Data presented in this report on the provision of services for victims of domestic abuse also show variations across areas and highlight that, whilst other agencies such as social care and health care services are already involved in the response to domestic abuse, such involvement is not widespread and more involvement from such agencies would help to improve victims' experiences.

How the Police can Help Domestic Problems

This flowchart explains how cases of domestic abuse are captured and flow through the criminal justice system. The data are not directly comparable, since they are collected on different bases (for example victims, crimes, suspects or defendants) and may not cover the same cohort because of variation in the time taken for cases to progress through the system.

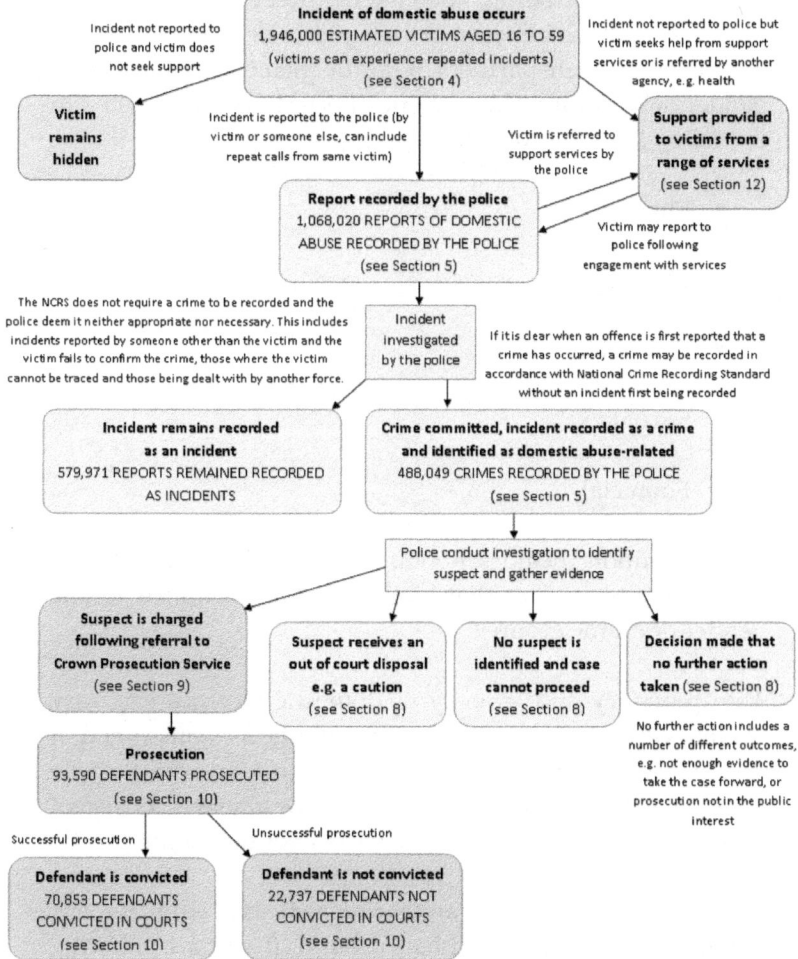

Fig 1: How data are captured and interlinked across the criminal justice system

What is domestic abuse?

Domestic abuse is categorised by any incident or pattern of incidents of controlling, coercive or threatening behaviour, violence or abuse between those aged 16 or over who are or have been intimate partners or family members regardless of gender or sexuality. This can encompass but is not limited to the following types of abuse:

- Physical

- Emotional

- Psychological

- Sexual

- Financial

This definition includes honour-based violence and forced marriage and is clear that victims are not confined to one gender or ethnic group.

The frequency and severity of domestic violence can vary dramatically, just one encounter counts as abuse, and it can be an ongoing pattern of behaviour. However, the one constant element of domestic abuse is the abuser's consistent efforts to maintain power and control over the victim.

Domestic abuse can affect anyone regardless of ethnicity, age, gender, sexuality or social background. If you are suffering from physical, sexual, psychological or financial abuse, or are being threatened, intimidated or stalked by a current or previous partner or close family member, it's likely you're a victim of domestic abuse.

You may be feeling frightened, isolated, ashamed or confused. If you have children it may be that they too are suffering, whether they witness abuse or not. Remember, you are not to blame for what is happening. You are not alone, and above all you do not have to suffer in silence – help is available.

Controlling behaviour

Controlling behaviour is a range of acts performed by the abuser and designed to make their victim subordinate and/or dependent. These acts include but are not limited to:

- Isolating the victim from sources of support

- Exploiting the victim's resources and capacities for personal gain

- Depriving the victim of the means needed for independence, resistance and escape

- Regulating the victim's everyday behaviour

Coercive behaviour

Coercive behaviour is an act or a pattern of acts of assault, threats, humiliation and intimidation or other abuse that is used by the abuser to harm, punish, or frighten their victim.

Physical abuse and sexual abuse

Physical abuse is the use of physical force against someone in a way that injures or endangers that person. The police have the power and authority to protect you from physical attack. Sexual abuse is a form of physical abuse. Forced sex, even by a spouse or intimate partner with whom you also have consensual sex, is an act of aggression and violence.

Emotional or psychological abuse

Just because you're not battered and bruised doesn't mean you're not being abused. Unfortunately, emotional abuse is often minimised or overlooked—even by the person being abused. Emotional abuse includes verbal abuse such as yelling, name-calling, blaming, and shaming. Isolation, intimidation, and controlling behaviour also fall under emotional abuse.

Honour-based violence

There is no honour in threatening or harming vulnerable people with violence. However, within London a small minority of both women and men experience violence and threats at the hands of their family or community in order to protect their perceived 'honour.' (Family members are defined as mother, father, son, daughter, brother, sister and grandparents, whether directly related, in-laws or step-family.)

There is nothing religious or cultural about this violence. It is a crime and we will take seriously any information received from any source relating to this subject.

If you are in fear of such violence or believe another may be suffering, do not underestimate the seriousness of the situation. Honour-based violence takes lives. By attending a police station or calling the Community Safety Unit for your borough you will be able to speak to an officer who can help.

The warning signs of honour-based violence are:

- Forms of communication being severed between victim and friends

- Withdrawal from education or workplace

- Criticism of victim for 'Western' adoption of clothing or make-up

- Restrictions in leaving the house or chaperoning outside the home

- Onset of depression or suicidal tendencies in an otherwise happy person

Go to our Contact us page and scroll to 'visit us' to find your nearest police station.

Forced marriage

We are committed to eradicating the practice of forced marriage. This is not to be confused with an arranged marriage, where parties involved have the choice to accept the arrangement or not. Forced marriage is when one party is threatened or bullied into making such a marriage. A family member might threaten suicide if the young person does not consent and in some cases the 'bride' or 'groom' take their own life rather than bring this perceived shame on the family by not entering such an agreement.

Forced marriage is an offence. If you are worried you might be forced into marriage or are worried for another, you are not alone. Please contact either the Forced Marriage Unit on 020 7008 0151 for advice or your local Community Safety Unit. We can offer victims a civil or criminal route to protect them from harm.

How to report domestic abuse

The Met Police's first priority is to protect you and any children you have. If the situation is an emergency an officer will attend and, if proportionate, necessary and lawful to do so, arrest the perpetrator, and take action to protect you from further harm - giving you time to think.

Report it

If you are a victim of domestic abuse, or know someone who is, and there is an emergency that is ongoing or life is in danger, dial 999.

If you have been the victim of domestic abuse, or are concerned for someone who is, you can report this in the safety of your local police station. If you require a translator, we can provide someone initially by phone and later in person.

In non-emergency cases and for general advice, please call 101.

How the Met can help straight away

Our officers will ensure that you are dealt with respectfully and spoken to away from the person responsible for the abuse. If you have been physically injured, it's important that your injuries are examined by a doctor. We will arrange medical care if necessary.

Staying in touch

The Police will stay in contact with you and see you through the whole investigation. Our aim is to contact you within 24 hours of you reporting the offence to let you know what's happening. We will also give you a dedicated phone number, so you can call us directly to find out how your case is going or talk about anything that might be worrying you.

In many cases, victims of domestic abuse require temporary or longer-term housing alternatives. It may be that you require an injunction to prevent the perpetrator approaching you, or perhaps need counselling or support. We work alongside highly trained non-police advisors who can assist with aftercare for you and your family.

Additionally, if you need to attend court for any reason there are support services available so that you do not feel overwhelmed or alienated by the legal process.

Clare's Law and requesting domestic violence offender data

The Domestic Violence Disclosure Scheme (DVDS) is often called 'Clare's Law' after the landmark case that led to it. Clare's Law gives any member of the public the right to ask the police if their partner may pose a risk to them. Under Clare's Law, a member of the public can also make enquiries into the partner of a close friend or family member.

The application process

Once an application is made, police and partner agencies will carry out a range of checks. If these reveal a record of abusive offences, or suggest a risk of violence or abuse, the police will consider sharing this information. Our aim is to help people to make a more informed decision on whether to continue a relationship and provide help and support when making that choice.

If we decide to make a disclosure, this will usually be made to the person at risk. This is unless, in the circumstances, someone else is better placed to use the information to protect them from abuse. There may be occasions when the police will not let you know whether a disclosure has or has not been made.

Any disclosure will be made in person - none of the disclosure is made in writing and you will not be given any documentation.

How to make an application under Clare's Law

To make an application you will need to attend a police station in person where a police officer or member of police staff will take the details of what prompted your enquiry. A safe means of contacting you will be established. You will need to give your name, address and date of birth.

We have described above the pinnacle of domestic violence,

the moment that control in both parties snaps if you do not recognise the situation keep reading as you may find that you are in the early stages of domestic violence. Domestic violence starts in a multitude of ways, the first tactic of the abuser will be to isolate the victim by controlling who he or she talks to thus building up a circle of friends who believe that the abuser is the most charming and kind person on earth. The arrival of children often escalates the violence as the controlling techniques of the abuser then have to extend to the children. Economic violence, abuse of money by either deprivation or over spending is a classic form of violence, he who controls the purse strings controls the family. Often sexual abuse will take place either by rape techniques, constant sexual demands or deprivation of sex in the hope that the other partner will seek solace elsewhere and thus be blamed for the break up. Sleep deprivation is a classic form of abuse, so often used by professional torturers.

Abusive relationships are dealt with in greater detail in Chapter 2

Once you realise that you are in an abusive relationship you must act very quickly. Do not worry about admitting to the Police that you are being abused, the Police have people from all walks of life and it is often the least likely people who are the abusers, judges' wives, Managing Directors' wives, husbands of eminent people through Policemen to the milkman's wife all seek help.

The abuser may have gained a respectable position in the PTA or council to cover up the true person, the abuser is usually charming to the outside world and particularly charming to those in authority.

It is unlikely that the Police or Social Services will intervene immediately in a marginal situation so to avoid the problem getting out of hand whilst the assessment of the parties is taking place we give below some tips on ways to control the abuser:

- Fighting back, a response to the assault may be a way to bring the abuser to his or her senses. A reaction means that he or she has lost total control over the victim. In cases of abuse against men, the first sign of a reaction from the woman usually results in a rash of false allegations against the man, resist these at all costs and issue a strict denial. In the case of male victims it is essential for the man not to hit here but to restrain the abuser.

- Challenging the control methods by talking to friends or taking a course.

- Persuade the abuser to go to counselling.

- Get a respected family or community member to challenge the abuser about the violence.

- Join a support group such as Victim Support, Women's Aid or Families Need Fathers. A group of kindred spirits breaks the isolation factor as when you realise that you are not alone you can face the problem.

- Call the Police, the majority of abusers will curb their actions with people in authority.

- Use Civil Law instruments such as Ouster Orders to restrain the abuser.

- The system may take against you if you are black, gay, lesbian or even male, do not worry you may have to suffer longer but a pattern of abuse usually emerges.

- If you are worried that your children are suffering abuse first talk to them about it and tell them how to avoid confrontation with the abuser. In cases where alcohol is present put them to bed before the abuser starts drinking. Immediately inform the Police Child Protection Unit and Social Services about your worries before the problem escalates.

- Once you understand your abuser you will be able to tackle the problem so know yourself first and steer away from outside quick fix solutions such as affairs or alcohol, you need all your wits about you as the abuser is usually one step ahead of you. Julian Nettlefold deals with Damage Limitation in his Chapter 9.

- **LASTLY AND NOT LEAST DOMESTIC VIOLENCE IS A CRIME AND THE PERPETRATORS OF IT CAN BE BROUGHT TO JUSTICE AND PROSECUTED.**

Met partner organisation support helplines

If you're experiencing domestic abuse, we can put you in touch with other support organisations that understand your specific needs. Below you'll find a list of organisations who can assist you as well as the Met.

The Met

Call the UK police non-emergency number, 101, if you need support or advice from the police and it is not an emergency.

Partner organisations

Women's Aid Domestic Violence Helpline
0808 2000 247
Free 24-hour national helpline run by Women's Aid and Refuge.

Men's Advice Line
0808 801 0327
Confidential helpline for male victims of domestic violence and abuse.

National Centre for Domestic Violence
0844 804 4999
A charity that specialises in providing you with assistance to obtain injunctions from being further abused.

Victim Support Service
0845 303 0900
National charity giving free and confidential help to victims of crime, witnesses, their family and friends.

Southall Black Sisters
020 8571 0800
Supports the needs of black (Asian and African-Caribbean) women.

Ashiana Project
020 8539 0427 or 020 8539 9656
Provides temporary, safe housing for South Asian, Turkish and Iranian women aged 16-30 experiencing domestic violence. Helps those who may be suffering from violence and threats of violence at the hands of their family or community (honour-based violence) or from forced marriage.

The Iranian and Kurdish Women's Rights Organisation
(IKWRO)
020 7920 6460
Provides assistance and support to Kurdish, Farsi and Arabic-speaking women living in London.

(Source: Met Police)

Chapter 9

Conciliation Confrontation

Hilary Halpin, Divorce Conciliation Service

The Denning Committee, reporting in 1947, first suggested that intervention by other parties than solicitors might help with the break down of marriages which were leading to divorce. They suggested *'whether a machinery should be set up for the purpose of attempting reconciliation between parties.'*

The Committee saw the preservation of marriage as a *'proper function of the State'* and persuaded the Home Office to make fairly substantial grants to the national Marriage Guidance Council for this purpose. It was made incumbent on solicitors to discuss with their clients the possibility of reconciliation and to certify whether they had done so. Sadly, this process, still in existence to-day, is more honoured in the breach than in the observance and has become nothing more than a formality with the solicitor signing a certificate stating that he has attempted to offer avenues of reconciliation.

The Finer Committee in 1974 proposed that there should be a new Family Court and recognised that whilst reconciliation was not a possibility for many couples, conciliation might help ease the pain of all concerned. They defined conciliation as:

'Assisting the parties to deal with the consequences of the established breakdown of their marriage, whether resulting in divorce or separation, by reaching agreements or giving consents or reducing the area of conflict upon custody, support, access to and education of the children.'

In 1975 a Working Party was set up by the Home Office to *'assemble information relating to marital problems and the provision of helping services.'* This Working Party reported in July 1978 with *'Marriage Matters, a consultative document.'* It was during the life of this Working Party that the first Conciliation Service was set up in Bristol and the Report mentioned it very favourably.

During the following three years several other services were started and currently there are about sixty services in England & Wales. Most of these agencies with the exception of a few run by Children's Charities such as Barnardos and the National Children's Home, were started on a shoe string and sadly as new agencies spring up others fall by the wayside because of shortage of finance. The Government has always refused to give grants to conciliation services while at the same time saying how useful they are. Clients who are legally-aided can get conciliation paid for but the reimbursement from Legal Aid to the agency is minimal.

Divorce, however it is looked at, from the couple's point of view, the children's point of view, or even the damage to the fabric of society as a whole, is a sad and painful business. The process of conciliation might justify its costs merely through the social benefits it brings, chiefly in relieving the distress of the children caught in divorce rows, let alone in the saving of legal fees.

The earlier agencies worked in different ways - depending often, on the background of their conciliators. Some agencies use only one conciliator, others two and the DCAS uses two conciliators, offering individual counselling for each partner and then a joint conciliation session with both partners and their two conciliators. The individual sessions provide an opportunity for the conciliators to assess how far the wish to separate has got, whether there is agreement between both partners that they are ready to go ahead with divorce.

Although it is essential that conciliators should be as even-handed as possible, there will be times when it is clear that one partner is very much more dominant than the other and is pressurising the partner who is not quite ready to accept the breakup. The obvious example being where one partner is a lawyer and can blind the other with their legal knowledge. If there is domestic violence present the abuser obviously has the dominant control over the other in the relationship discussions.

It is always important to try and keep the focus on the child's needs, returning to this every time when one or other client wants to go back to recriminate over the past. Asking the parents to describe their children is often a help. Most parents want to be *'good parents'* and given the chance they will suddenly become warm and animated, inviting the other partner to agree with them and it is clear for a few minutes that they have shared great pleasure.

Whilst there will always be couples who can acknowledge that the marriage is over, that they should release each other from a dead marriage and make as satisfactory arrangements as possible, the majority who come for conciliation have not been able to talk together about their unhappiness for a long time.

There are husbands and wives who have found a new partner and may have been living a double life for months, or even several years and who would have let this go on if the new partner had not wanted more from the relationship or if, with time, he or she had not become careless. Suddenly the hair line fracture in the marriage becomes a large break and the grass on the other side looks greener. Where men are in this situation, wives often say that he is *'not the man they married'*, but it is the same man, only he has to build a shell around him to avoid tears and emotions *'unmanning him'*.

There are also the men who do not want a divorce. They thought they were good husbands and fathers; some being the *'new man'* who takes a share in the household chores and child minding. Others at each end of the social scale, are still old fashioned parents who see themselves as earning the family income, leaving for work each morning and returning, perhaps to read a bedtime story to the children or help with homework before sitting down to a well cooked meal with a couple of hours afterwards to read, watch TV or go to the pub. Suddenly like a bolt from the blue they lose their wife, their children and their home and have to pay for it!

There are wives who are also taken by surprise. They very often, had a good job and intended to return to it later when the children were older. They are well aware that they would have dropped several steps on the ladder they had already climbed. Like so many of the men who thought they were good fathers, the women felt they were good wives and mothers. Maybe there was a small vacuum there which needed to be filled but it didn't seem very big. Suddenly some other woman, possibly younger, possibly a colleague at work reached out and claimed her husband. It may well have been that the marriage had been dying for a long time and she hadn't noticed it because running a home and rearing children is a very time consuming occupation; rejection is very painful. Her status in the community is as a married woman and added to all her other feelings of hurt and anger, is shame. It is very difficult to face the fact that you are not wanted.

Some mothers faced with this rejection see the children as the only weapons they have. They refer constantly to *'my child'* and start to give instructions as to who they may see when they are with their father. They limit telephone calls and try to control them by hovering in the background. They will say the child was upset on return from a contact visit and find it difficult to understand that children feel they must assuage and pander to the parent with whom they are living.

The situation is often exacerbated by the fact that there is a new partner. If there is not one initially things can be reasonably manageable, depending on the circumstances of the split, but can blow up if one appears.

It is so essential for the mother to understand the importance of the father in the child's life. Research has shown that children who have easy and frequent contact with their fathers do better at school, are happier in adolescence and make better relationships as they grow older. It is often difficult for mothers to accept this concept while they are feeling angry.

In 1978 the Judge in the case of M v M said:

> *"The companionship of a parent is in any ordinary circumstances of such immense value to the child that for my part I would prefer to call it a basic right of the child rather than of the parent."*

He went onto say,

> *"that no child should be deprived of this right unless the Court is wholly satisfied that such access should cease and that is a conclusion at which a Court should be extremely slow to arrive."*

In the middle of all this unhappiness are the children. They have felt for some time that something was wrong; they still feel loved and wanted but their security is very shaky. The parents who could be relied on to mend the broken toy or replace the button missing from Teddy's eye are in turmoil themselves.

Conciliators try to help parents explain to the children what is happening, although Mummy and Daddy no longer want to live together they have every intention of continuing as parents. This can help the children to accept that their father is not going to move out of their lives. (NB although in reality the majority of absent fathers lose contact with their children within two years.) It also reassures them that they are not the cause of the unpleasant vibes which were drifting about. Children very often feel that they have caused the trouble, that if they weren't there it wouldn't have happened. This feeling can be increased when the parents row over the methods of child rearing.

Throughout it is important to stress that we are talking about a child's right to have two parents; that they are not '*my child*' but '*our child*' and it is his or her needs we are considering. Mothers generally take it for granted that they will get the Residence Order if the case goes to Court. It is sometimes helpful with a mother who is exceptionally rigid about contact to put it to her that the other alternative would be that her husband should get the Residence Order and she should have contact. While this is unlikely to happen, 95% of mothers get Residence Orders, it does sometimes make the mothers stop and reconsider. (NB: It is sad to note that although the Children's Act allows for a Joint Residence Order to be made, that is the child spending 50% of its time with both parents, very few have in fact been made and are regarded as '*disruptive*' to the children)

Not all conciliation sessions achieve the results that conciliators would like, some cases will really only be settled in Court despite the fact that the couple would have done better to give and take more generously.

Sometimes an arrangement for contact is worth trying out, the couple returning in two or three months to see if it needs re-thinking.

Out-of-Court conciliation allows for this kind of trial and error adjustments being made.

Conciliation is hard work and while the importance of it is to facilitate the children having contact with both parents, unless the feelings of anger, hurt and often revenge are sorted out they continue long after the divorce, spoiling the future relationships of the adults and, more importantly, damaging the children.

Case Study – Access

When anger boils over to excess and your ex-wife attempts
to stop all contact due to argument or conflict, beware. This
conflict may be deliberately manufactured to stop all contact
to the children by a six month cooling off recommendation
from the court or solicitor. Once this six month period is over
the mother may make a further application to the court that
as the father you have not seen your children for six months
you have neglected your access rights. At times where you
see your partner becoming agitated or make unreasonable
demands have as little contact with her as possible and when
dropping the children off at her home say nothing to her and
correspond by letter on important matters if necessary. If the
matter is still unresolved don't forget you have recourse to
the courts for a specific issue or prohibitive steps application.
It is an offence to deny access laid down by the Court and
whereas only one women in twenty years has gone to gaol for
this offence it a strong enough threat to use on your ex-wife.
If the children are worried by any behaviour by your ex-wife
tell Social Services immediately as she may have developed a
stress related illness or clinical depression or alcoholism due
to the strain of the divorce process or a previous condition.

Chapter 10

Damage Limitation, Some Helpful Hints

Julian Nettlefold

'A separated parent feels excluded from the child's life and this is usually coupled with hostility towards the carer.'
Childright

This chapter is designed to give a *'personal touch'* to the book. There are so many professional people giving you advice, I described it to someone like slipping down a greasy tube. Here are some hints to help with such problems as residence, money, job, health, friends, access, records and your own psychology. Seeking a remedy through legal channels is your last resort but you must be aware of the consequences of going to law at an early stage of any marital problems.

1. Home and Away

If your wife's family lives abroad and you see signs of unrest, official looking letters, frequent calls from the family, different clothes being bought, the first action to take is to confront your wife with your worries. Try and sort the situation out amicably before you entertain seeing a solicitor.

Failing that you must put your wife's passport in a safe place as if she is confused and not thinking straight she may well make an impulsive move without thinking it through. Although it is easy to get are placement the reaction gained from her not being able to find it will be enough to justify your fears. If you are convinced that she is about to leave, see a solicitor and prepare an injunction to stop her going. Before doing this make sure that the solicitor understands the situation, do not accept any delay.

You must realise that if this part of the proceedings is handled wrongly then what follows will ultimately be divorce. You can serve an injunction without divorce papers or in most cases you will be advised to serve the papers with the divorce petition. If you serve the injunction with the divorce petition you have already put the wheels of divorce in motion.

Case Study - Richard

Richard had been happily married for ten years when problems began to happen in his marriage. His wife was South American and he was worried that she would go back there with the children. He consulted a lawyer and told him his fears, the lawyer delayed serving the injunction. The wife left the country with the children and Richard went to South America to see them. He was denied access to his wife and both she and her mother assaulted him when he came to the home. He has not seen his children for eleven years.

His wife subsequently remarried a rich German who

was then accused by her of sexually assaulting her child

He committed suicide, Richard has still not seen his children despite Court Orders in both the UK and South America allowing access.

Case Study - John

John was happily married until the arrival of his daughter when he noticed a severe change in his wife who had family in The Republic of Ireland. He contacted a professional child care lawyer on a Friday who advised him to take his child away to a friend over the week-end while the injunction was being prepared. He told his wife and took the child away. During the week-end he rang his wife from a call box to say that everything was all right. During the call a Police car drew up and bundled him and his fifteen month old child in. He was separated from his child for several hours and despite giving the number of his solicitor the Police refused to believe him about his wife's condition; he was charged with abduction. His wife arrived picked up the child and went to Ireland. His solicitor could do nothing about it, he now sees his daughter twice a year.

2. Money

A sudden drop in family living standards causes great turmoil within the family and is recognised as being one of the biggest contributors towards divorce. If you have monetary problems tackle them quickly, tell your wife and cut down on all unnecessary expenses. Don't hide the problem, it will not go away but your wife and children may well.

You will find as the whole problem emerges that you will require a great deal of money to pay legal bills, doctors' bills and general household bills necessary to *'keep the peace.'* Create a budget for each expense and if you can discuss with your wife the best way to spend and save.

If the relationship has deteriorated to such an extent that all trust has gone consider increasing the mortgage, if that is impossible create a fighting fund in a separate account. As soon as divorce proceedings start your wife's solicitors will put a matrimonial order on your home which will freeze any chance you have of selling the property or raising money against it. We will deal with the effect divorce has on your job and business later.

Try and be as reasonable as possible to your wife during the traumas and pay her money for upkeep of her and the children. Do not be over generous, as it will not reflect in any eventual financial settlement which could be two years away. Money can disappear quickly in these situations; money management is essential.

3. Your Career & Business

After financial problems, business and job problems are a major cause of disruption. The loss of a job means loss of esteem and money; it also means that the father will be around the house a lot more. Try and keep active and spend some time away from the house.

Discuss the problem with your wife and family it may be only temporary.

In circumstances when a matrimonial order is placed on the house and where you are self-employed or using the house as a bank guarantee, under 'Clayton's Case' the bank is unable to advance you any more money under all existing loan arrangements. If you are self-employed and unable to provide any other form of security and your business is not going well there is a definite possibility that you will have to cease trading.

During this traumatic time you will not be able to concentrate 100% on work, explain to your clients and employers that you are going through problems they will understand as many of them will have been there as well.

If self-employed make sure all your records are up to date as they will be needed to negotiate any financial settlement.

4. Your Health

Your health will inevitably suffer, eat well, don't drink too much, go to bed early and don't party to escape the problem, you will need the money later. There will be a large degree of uncertainty and strain, the day to day negotiations with solicitors will take up a lot of your time and energy. Try not to be bad tempered and short with people either on the telephone or at work, you will find that your character will be changed dramatically due to the increased stress.

You will either be living with your wife and children under the same roof or living with friends or alone. You will find great periods of remorse and tears; although it is a great temptation don't take to the bottle, it will do you no good. Although it is trying for friends and family try and pour your heart out to someone as to bottle it up may cause psychological or physical problems later. Counselling is essential, without counselling you face illness or suicide. Don't forget that 12 times as many divorced men commit suicide than women.

It is vital that you go for counselling as the right counsellor can ease the hardship. Hilary Halpin deals with this in Chapter 9.

The main thing to remember is that one day it will end.

It will never happen to me, it will, it happened to Charles.

Case Study - Charles

Charles had been happily married for fifteen years when his wife asked him to leave the house. He had lovely children and went to live in London. Six weeks later he committed suicide. No one could understand why until it emerged that his wife had a lover. She had a baby by the lover but will not marry him as changing her name will result in the loss of her widow's pension from Charles. The baby's name is being changed by deed poll.

5. Friends, Relations, Relationships

The old adage that you will fall in love quickly and remarry does not always stand. Unless you are having a relationship started before the break up beware of starting another quickly. You may soon discover that you are walking along the same road. You will find that you may become scared of getting involved and run as soon as she becomes keen, explain the situation early on. It will take you a minimum of two years to take the emotion out of the situation. If you were the partner who walked out the guilt will live with you for even longer. You will find yourself boring your friends to tears over the divorce if they are good friends they will listen if not you may find a shortage of invitations. Some friends and family may take the other partner's side, don't worry it happens all the time and it may be many years before they will see you again or even understand why it happened. Don't rubbish your wife in public it will do you no good and you will probably find that she is being a great deal more subtle in her dealings with friends and family. Try not to bore your friends with the problems - you will lose them. Confide in a selected few and if possible they can act as intermediaries.

6. Keeping Records

As soon as you suspect that there are problems start a diary of events. This will be crucial when you are talking to doctors and lawyers. Always remember to keep every scrap of paper relevant to your problem. If necessary tape record conversations to give as evidence to the behaviour. You will find that professional people need a lot of convincing when female behavioural problems occur.

Always keep a diary during the crisis this will help all the professional involved, especially in cases of PND or PMS as a behaviour pattern can be established and the problem solved. If you are going for a residence order for your children make sure these notes are clear and concise they may make or break a case.

7. Abduction

You may reach a stage of exasperation with your family situation and decided to take your children away from the problem - DON'T.

The Child Abduction Act rendered it a criminal offence for one parent to remove a child from the country without the other's consent or the court's leave. The 1985 Child Abduction & Custody Act enables the child to be returned by the co-operation of the central authorities of the country concerned. If the proceedings begin within one year of the abduction then the child must be returned; after a year the child is deemed to have settled in his or her new environment. In 1991 numbers of abductions reached 1000. The authorities in the UK have been criticised for not taking more preventative measures under the Children Act. Certain prevention measures are in force such as putting a block on the issue of duplicate birth certificates, stopping the ordinary passport and non-issue of visitor's passports to children under eight years old. In extreme cases airport and port authorities can be notified. If the country is a signatory of the Hague Convention the parent is at liberty to return immediately. In essence this does not happen; time and time again mothers remove their children from the country and no action is taken by the father's solicitors to have the children returned.

Don't forget that once they have gone then you will almost certainly never see your children again.

If a father removes the children instant moves are made to have the child returned as in the recent Malkin case where a little known fact is that his wife initially removed Oliver from the matrimonial home to France & later denied Peter access.

8. **Charities & Self-Help Groups**

In cases where children are involved, under the present system, 95% of residence orders are given to the mother. As a man this is a very difficult situation to face and in many cases is made more complicated by denial of access by the mother.

Charities such as Families Need Fathers and DADS are available to help men in situations. The cost of joining is low compared to approx. £100.00 per hour for a solicitor.

Not only will you be able to air the problems of your case in front of men who have been in similar situations but you will also be given the morale boost that there are men out there in much worse situations. The knowledge and advice which can be gained from these organisations is immeasurable and should be used. Certainly in my case had I met FNF at the start of my divorce the outcome could have been remarkably different for both myself and Harry.

9. Nature & Nurture

We are all born with in-built role models which may stretch back centuries. These role-models lead us to be attracted to certain characteristics in a person, you may come from a family of alcoholic abusers, child abusers, people with bad tempers. These traits often are exacerbated by the arrival of children and cause the sudden personality change that so many men describe. Your partner may also be scared and confused at this sudden increase in personality change and will often try and hide it as it may be reminiscent of something in her family she was trying to block out. Very often depression, alcoholism and stress disorders will occur suddenly and without warning.

Try and encourage your partner to seek help from Relate or a psychologist. If she won't go, go yourself as you will find out that either you may be the cause of the problem in which case try and change or he will help you how to live with the situation until the storm is over. My own divorce revealed a fault in my family structure which when I was able to stand back and look had been as clear as daylight for many years. I had been treated in exactly the same way as my maternal & paternal grandfathers. My mother and my ex-wife had similar behavioural characteristics, I had been attracted to these in spite of the fact that swore I would never marry someone who argued. I have been subjected to a family especially a brother who thrives on long & involved arguments.

My psychologist first pointed out this attract-ion to my wife as a result of family similarities.

I was subconsciously used to her behaviour. Strangely it was not until after my divorce that I discovered the true toxic nature of my family. I followed my psychologist's advice and tried out his theory. I had known a girl for many years and fancied her a great deal, she had been married to a friend of mine and divorced after seven years. I rang a friend for her number who warned me of her instability. I told him not to worry and saw her over a period of seven months. One afternoon during a telephone call she went berserk, I quietly put the receiver down and whispered a quiet prayer of thanks to the psychologist.

Case Study- Peter

I had the greatest pleasure in meeting Peter at a New Year's party in Scotland. During our conversation it became quite apparent that he had suffered the same problems as myself. *"I married two like yours,"* he said. *"I thought drugs would help and they didn't."* He was divorced and living on nothing. Two months later he walked into a London hospital A&E Department died there of a severe infection largely due to stress at 52 years old.

In conclusion the way of coping with an unexpected and confusing situation in your marriage is to stand back and look at the problem as if you were an outsider. The advice I had was to write everything down and take the emotion out of the problem. Once you can look at the subject objectively you will achieve a lot objectively. Emotions and uncertainty will only fuel the fire of the eventual family destruction.

Case Study – Bill

Bill was happily married to Liz. She was larger than life and Bill liked her strong attitude to life. Bill was an engineer and he was posted to Pakistan when his wife's behavioural problems began. She would attack him and the children and become uncontrollable exhibiting epileptic type symptoms. They were posted back to Britain and he came to me in an exasperated state and said that she was now totally out of control and that she had served divorce papers suggesting that he was a transvestite, a homosexual and had molested the children. He explained that his wife had a goitre which was going to be operated on. At the Court case he lost both his homes and was granted limited access to his children. He was told that on no account could he appeal before the case! He said to me that both he and his wife were on tricyclic drugs for malaria and I discovered that these had unknowingly helped her problem, we also found that thyroid problems cause behavioural problems. His lawyers had not defended the accusations of sexual deviancy and indeed had evidence to the contrary. They had also failed to bring into account the effects of the goitre. Bill was denied the right to appeal, it seems likely that if the case had been dealt with properly a sensible separation could have been achieved if that was indeed necessary.

Case Study – Geoff

Geoff came from a family with a very domineering father and Geoff had inherited these characteristics. But Geoff was a very loving and caring father and had no idea until too late that his wife Margaret had been seeing a psychiatrist after the birth of their son Tom. Geoff said that he would go to Wales to set up a new family business and six months later Margaret would follow. Margaret did follow but only to tell Geoff that their marriage was over. Geoff subsequently found out that she had been seeing a psychiatrist for some years and that he had been singled out as the cause. Geoff's temper had got worse over the problem and confusion and thought that the period of separation might solve the problem; they are now divorced but Geoff has generous access. The legal problems were all sorted out amicably.

It was only many years later that I found the real and harrowing reason for their divorce. Margaret came from a toxic family where her father had been sexually abusing her and her brother and others. Geoff was also from a toxic family but was the abuser. Margaret remarried but that was a disaster as did Geoff who seems happily married. Margaret's father's activities were never unmasked.

Chapter 11

Preparing Yourself for Your Lawyer

Julian Nettlefold

*'A lawyer has no business with the justice or injustice of the case
he undertakes, unless his client asks his opinion, and then he is
bound to give it honestly. The justice or the injustice of the case is
to be decided by the Judge.'*
Dr Samuel Johnson 1709-1784

To understand the true role your lawyer will play in your
decision to seek a divorce we must look back in history to
examine the workings of the legal system. The specialist
divorce firm's origins lie in the breakaway divorce teams
which formed a small part of their law firm's litigation
department. The huge growth in the divorce rates coupled to
the explosion in incomes and property prices since 1985 has
resulted in the creation of the large specialist divorce firms
with a large number of partners and staff. A total bill of over
£2 million, is not unknown in extreme circumstances. The
workings of the Legal System are based on an adversarial
system of two powerful teams of lawyers slogging it out to
the death in a Court of Law to win the Case for their client;
divorce is no different. The founders of the eminent divorce
firms had their roots in this system and thus confrontation
and adversity is second nature to them. The High Court Judges

themselves were practising barristers in the late sixties and seventies where the stereotype role of the mother as the main carer and the father as the aggressive bully were prominent. Their views were reinforced by Government policy stating that as the man is the bread winner of the family in most cases the children should remain with the mother to enable the family to survive financially. This policy is further reinforced by financial constraints of the Legal Aid system; should a level playing field be available to enable men to gain custody of their children then the Legal Aid bill would soar by a factor of ten. London is now the capital for the high profile divorce case where both partners sordid requests and demands are aired in public all over the tabloids with no regard to the effect this has on their children, its all about money.

It has now been recognised that the adversarial system is not necessarily the answer and the Children Act of 1989 and the Green Paper on divorce in 1993 and the 1996 Family Law Act, underlined the importance that the children of the marriage must be foremost in the Court's mind. Having said this the Children Act still slants the balance in favour of the mother by stating (Part 1 (f)) that the caring capabilities of each parent should be taken into account when a decision is made as to residence. The growth in the number of women working full time is now gradually leading to the belief that men could be and in some cases are the best carer. Here it is up to men to prove that the perception that the Judges have of their gender is wrong.

The overall aim of the Children Act was to change the current attitude within the system, this is brought out by a clause (1 Sub section 5) which states that rather than making the wrong order the Court should make no order at all if it is better for the children.

146

It is essential to understand the *'nature of the beast'* before embarking on your decision to divorce. A divorce lawyer must not be regarded as a mediator or a psychologist, his role is to create the legal arrangements for his client in his or her best interest. He will never meet your partner thus his perception of the case will always be based on what you tell him and what he is told by the other side's lawyer. Considerations are now being aired that perhaps it is wrong that a lawyer cannot represent both parties as he will have far better grasp of the case by meeting both parties. In many cases of alcoholism, depression and stress the person concerned will be in denial and blaming everyone else but themselves, the divorce lawyer is an ideal victim in this situation as his charter is to work in the best interests of his client in a situation where he will not be able to seek an opinion from the other partner.

If you do not like the advice given by the lawyer you are quite at liberty to go elsewhere but it is essential that before considering visiting another solicitor you must be clear in your own mind what is required from the situation and whether your thoughts are rational. As far as the lawyer is concerned he is dealing with another case and he will deal with it as to his firm's general code of practice. The lawyer's main aim should be to arrive at a conclusion which is in the best interests of the family, but this is not always the case.

Your choice of lawyer may have come by word of mouth, by recommendation, from a doctor or from another lawyer. Each firm has its own fingerprint of operation and the other side will have a good idea of your partner's intentions by his or her choice of legal firm. The Solicitors Family Law Association has been set up to provide a specialist service in divorce for the family, but its operation still remains adversarial.

In a great majority of cases the lawyer will create an atmosphere of adversity and actively encourage accusations. He or she may well try to instigate ouster proceedings to remove the other partner from the house, he may recommend accusing your partner of sexual abuse to your children, he may recommend denial of all access to your partner, it is up to you and your lawyer to counter these allegations. The best advice should be to arrive at an outcome which will enable you to have some future contact and discussion with your partner, don't forget you still have school functions and weddings to attend together. The 1993 Green Paper encourages parents to seek a solution by negotiation outside the Court.

We must now examine the person at the other side of the desk, the lawyer. When the appointment is made, you will believe that you are the only person in the world getting divorced and that he must give you 100% of his time. He has probably seen six or seven people before you, been in Court all day the day before and dealt with hundreds of people like yourself over the years he has been a lawyer. As the song goes *'first impressions are lasting impressions,'* at the first meeting the lawyer will have a good idea as to your character, intentions and feelings towards your partner and children. He will discuss your marriage and your partner, has a baby just been born and therefore there may be a possibility of Post Natal Depression, has the partner lost his or her job, is your job creating a lot of stress on the family.

Should there be an indication that medical professionals have been involved before that person has come to the lawyer then their detailed opinion must be obtained to give the lawyer a clearer understanding as to the situation he is dealing with. A lawyer in no way should be regarded as an expert in anything else than the law. He will assess whether the marriage is salvable and his first move should be to recommend a conciliator to work for both parties. This is not always the case and in most cases due to pressure of work, the individual concerned or company policy the lawyer will recommend immediate legal action. If legal action is recommended an immediate decision is not required and not recommended. On no account be bullied into making the wrong decision, you are the client and you issue the instructions.

Many lawyers have had cases in which they are almost certain at the first meeting that their client did not want a divorce and it has been the case that in spite of going through the process of laying down the structure for that divorce, the event in some cases never comes to fruition.

The lawyer's other job will be to take the *'pricks'* out of the situation with the other party's solicitor in order to arrive at a level judgement. In the majority of cases both parties are in a very emotional state and the actions taken by either of them may have been fully justified given the circumstances. Once the lawyer is appointed be sure that he explains the financial implications of your decision and whether you are really in a position to fight the case as you have put it. After the ritual of the exchange of letters and cheques he will then contact your partner's solicitors and they will begin the long dialogue. Make sure that you are informed of every letter and conversation made to give you an element of control in the matter. As in all professions the degree of commitment to a case varies from firm to firm and can range from the quick fix divorce, that is clean the husband out and take the money to a structured situation to enable the family to at least exist in a future situation which will enable some form of communication.

But in a number of cases the situation arises where you have a vindictive partner who will do anything in his or her power to destroy the other party either financially, emotionally or both. Here you have to come to a very critical decision, do you fight this person or walk away from a situation, which is bound to damage the children, and take second best.

It must be in the best interests of both parties and their children to come to an agreement to save the huge costs and the time involved.

Your children will treat you with far more respect if you can go to them with hand on heart and say that you have both worked out a situation which will suit everybody; they do not want to see mummy and daddy fighting for the rest of their lives.

Check list:

1. Prepare yourself before your meeting with a list of events and questions.

2. Make sure that your lawyer has a particular speciality in your problem be it medical, financial or children, if he does not go to another.

3. Make sure if you appoint him that he confirms his fee and terms in writing before any work is done.

4. Keep him up to speed and prevent delay or time waste.

5. Ensure that all aspects of the case especially any violence against you is kept in affidavits.

6. Prevent any out of Court Settlements without the particular legal document required such as the Rule 76a Statement as in ancillary relief.

7. Don't forget that in all divorce cases especially when children are involved you are always free to return to Court should you disagree with the judgement.

8. f faced with any ouster or sexual allegation issue strict denials if they are untrue and on no account settle theses by consent. (see case study below)

9. Insist on attending the Section 41 appointment for the children's arrangements.

10. If you are not happy with your lawyer change.

At the end of proceedings always demand a fee breakdown

Case Study - Freddie

Freddie is a very successful banker. After several years of a very happy marriage with three lovely children he was promoted to managing director.

Up until then his wife had been quite content to have the odd function once a week but the pressure of Freddie becoming MD became so great that his wife could not take the strain and filed for divorce. Luckily the lawyer in question spotted the true reason for the breakdown and although the couple went through the process of separating and obtaining the Decree Nisi, after three years when Freddie was no longer MD they were back together again living in the country.

It is a sad reflection that after years of debate and the formulation of the failed 1990 Family Law Act that Parliament has had to revisit the problems of divorce. In my view the Family Law Act and the introduction of *'No Fault Divorce,'* was more to protect the lawyer from being sued rather than solve the problems in the Family Courts and the costs to society and our children.

It would be impossible to cover all aspects of Family Law as the system is on a continual rate of change as the latest attempts to change the system emerge in 2018. So please use this Chapter as a guide and not as legal advice.

Index